DIA LOG UES

— ON —
THE REFUGEE CRISIS

SPARK HOUSE

Printed in the United States

24 23 22 21 20 19 18   1 2 3 4 5 6 7 8

ISBN 9781506448602

Written by Halima Z. Adams, Brianne Casey, Aubrey Leigh Grant, Sarah Krause, Beth Oppenheim-Chan, Matthew Soerens, Jenny Yang
Edited by Carla Barnhill
Cover design by Joe Reinke
Art Direction by Joe Reinke
Interior Design by Joe Reinke
Copyediting by Heidi Mann
Proofreading by Alena Schuessler DeYoung

DIALOGUES ON THE REFUGEE CRISIS

Sparkhouse team: Carla Barnhill, Bryan Bliss, Aaron Christopher, Julie Coffman, Erin Gibbons, Kristofer Skrade, Josh Stifter, Erik Ullestad, Jeremy Wanek, Christopher Zumski Finke

Unless otherwise noted, all Scripture quotations are from the New Revised Standard Version of the Bible, Copyright ©1989 by the Division of Education of the National Council of Churches of Christ in the United States of America. Used by permission. All rights reserved.

Library of Congress Control Number: 2018942324

PUBLISHED BY SPARKHOUSE
510 Marquette Avenue
Minneapolis, MN 55402
wearesparkhouse.org

TABLE OF CONTENTS

FOREWORD

WHO IS MY NEIGHBOR?

I distinctly remember sitting in a third-floor classroom overlooking the college quad when a friend made an announcement to the class that set my life on a new course. She'd recently begun volunteering with World Relief, a refugee resettlement agency with an office down the street from our campus, and had become close friends with a family who had come to the United States as refugees from Rwanda. This family had an adolescent son, Denis, and my friend thought he might benefit from having a male mentor. She wondered if any of us would be interested. Playing basketball and soccer with a twelve-year-old sounded like something I could handle, so I signed up.

In short order, Denis and his family became my close friends. As I did my best—imperfectly, to be sure—to help them walk through the adjustment to a new culture, language, and school system, they became my tutors in the refugee experience. Denis had been born shortly before genocide broke out in Rwanda in 1994. His family escaped to Tanzania, then migrated to the Democratic Republic of Congo, and ultimately found safety in Zambia, where they lived for roughly a decade. Eventually, after being among the lucky few to be carefully vetted and selected, they were resettled to the United States.

When I finished college and needed to find a place to live, I rented an apartment in the complex where Denis and his family lived. The apartments didn't look particularly impressive—they were a bit shabby and had some serious pest control problems—but thanks to the people living there, I quickly found it to be a uniquely vibrant community. I was swiftly embraced by neighbors, most of them former refugees who hailed from more than a dozen countries of origin.

I tried to be a good neighbor, helping kids do their homework and adults decipher their mail. These families would more than repay me in delicious Rwandan, Somalian, Burmese, and Iranian food. Some evenings I ate three meals, moving from apartment to apartment at the invitation of various neighbors. I gained weight—and a deep admiration for the resilience and courage of my new friends, whose life experiences had been so radically different—and much more difficult—than mine, but who also had a lot more in common with me than I might have guessed.

My proximity to these neighbors made me want to learn more about the countries and conflicts they had been forced to flee. My heart broke as they told me of their loved ones still languishing in refugee camps or struggling to make ends meet as urban refugees. I began reading books and watching documentaries to try to better understand the geopolitical dynamics that had contributed to global refugee crises over the decades. And I found myself wrestling with how, in some cases, my country's foreign policies had either helped or harmed the situation.

Interacting with these new friends also changed how I read the Bible. Suddenly I couldn't read the Scriptures without noticing how many heroes of the biblical narrative were forced across a national border by the threat of persecution or violence. Though I was raised in the church and thought of myself as biblically literate, I'd somehow missed the scores of biblical injunctions related to welcoming, loving, and seeking justice for vulnerable foreigners.

Over the past several years, as refugee issues have come to the forefront of political discussions in the United States and around the world, I've become increasingly convinced that the church has a vital role to play in responding to a global refugee crisis. Too often, though, I fear Christians have come to think about the refugee crisis only as a political, economic, or cultural issue, and have failed to reckon with our responsibilities as followers of Jesus to recognize each refugee as an individual made in the image of God, as a neighbor whom Jesus commands us to love as we love ourselves.

As US refugee policies have changed, some of my former refugee neighbors' hopes for reunification with family members still overseas have been deferred or dashed entirely by travel bans and the gradual erosion of the US refugee resettlement program. I've lamented and grieved, fearful that our country is stepping back precisely at the time when we as a nation, as faith communities, and as individuals need to step forward, to rise up.

That's why I'm so grateful you're engaging this powerful learning resource. Bringing their unique perspectives from many years of direct experience, the various authors in this book explain the history of churches' engagement with refugees, the global dynamics of forced displacement, and the policy issues that directly impact the lives of refugees. They explore how the resettlement process works for the small share of the world's refugees offered the opportunity to be resettled to the United States, address some of the historic undercurrents that have shaped our attitudes about refugees, and consider how faith communities in the US can help refugees not only resettle, but thrive.

My prayer for you is that, at the conclusion of this study, you would be not merely better informed, but you and your congregation would be equipped and inspired to respond in ways guided by Jesus' call to welcome the stranger—and that in doing so, you would find, as I have, that these "strangers" become neighbors and ultimately family.

—Matthew Soerens
    United States Director of Church Mobilization, World Relief

1

THE STORY WE LIVE IN

THE HISTORY OF THE CHURCH'S RESPONSE TO REFUGEES

BY BRIANNE CASEY

With more than 65.5 million people displaced in the world today, no one can dispute that we are in the midst of a refugee crisis. For most of us in the United States, the crisis has been characterized by media images of overcrowded boats traveling tenuously across the Mediterranean, lines of migrant families crossing borders, and seas of white tents crowded into refugee camps. These images and the people and complex conflicts behind them evoke a broad range of emotional responses—fear, compassion, resignation. While the images are real and important, they can also blur our understanding of both what this crisis is about and how we might respond in meaningful ways. For those who see such images and find their hearts moved, there can be a tendency to be so overwhelmed with emotion that they are unable to act. For those who find themselves anxious, afraid, or even angry at the thought of refugees coming to their own country, the sheer number of people represented in the images can reinforce their fears about what will be asked of countries that offer aid. Even among Christians, there is a resistance to reaching out to refugees. A 2016 survey by LifeWay Research reports that only 8 percent of Protestant churches were assisting refugees in their local community at the time.[1]

Yet, as Christians—as human beings—we can't turn away from the suffering of others. It is the call of the church in our time to overcome our own fears and biases in order to determine how best to address this growing crisis. It's an opportunity to explore our history as the body of Christ and the ways in which the church has responded to the needs of refugees. The challenges facing refugees, as well as communities seeking to help them, are many and deserve our honest and thoughtful attention—even when it's overwhelming, even when it pushes us outside of what's comfortable. Moving beyond the complex emotions of the current crisis and focusing on facts doesn't lessen the impact of this issue; it sharpens it by providing a more accurate, intelligent, and actionable response—the kind of response the world needs.

"ACTION AS SHALL JUSTIFY FAITH"

The last time the world faced a refugee crisis of this size was the World War II era, when more than 40 million Europeans were displaced.[2] At that time, far fewer structures and organizations were in place than today to respond to displacement at a global level. Into that deficit stepped the church, which was able to respond in ways the government could not.

One of the initial elements of response was to acknowledge what was happening half a world away. Leading up to the war, church voices mounted, urging acknowledgment of the human rights abuses in Nazi Germany and underscoring the need to offer assistance to those fleeing the situation. In 1936, the Baptist Observer's single editorial urged American churches to pray for and welcome refugees. Public awareness sharply increased with the international reporting and images of Kristallnacht, or the Night of Broken Glass, when over 250 synagogues and 7,000 Jewish-owned businesses were destroyed in November 1938.[3] Fifty-three prominent church leaders signed a 1939 petition in support of admitting 20,000 German refugee children to the United States, saying that "[Sympathies], however deep, are not enough ... these must translate themselves into action as shall justify faith."[4] The newly unified Methodist Church urged individuals and churches to assist refugees of any faith. The 1939 Presbyterian General Assembly referenced "common morality and decency" in responding to the crisis.[5] Although the growth of widespread awareness and advocacy was slow, as the war continued, the church's prayers did turn to action.

Immigration laws at the time admitted only people with the financial means to support themselves—those not likely to become "public charges." But most war refugees had long since lost possessions and wealth due to Nazi policies. So when President Truman's directive allowed for "corporate affidavits"—essentially, pledges from US organizations to guarantee financial support for refugees—at least 2,500 were submitted by church organizations.[6] In 1948, US churches agreed to resettle 60,000 individuals.[7] Several denominations also established organizations to support refugees arriving in large cities. The Episcopal Church established the Episcopal Committee on German Refugees with a staff serving displaced persons arriving in New York City. The National Lutheran Council, which had been established to serve World War I refugees, also provided assistance in New York City.[8] Other faith-based refugee-serving organizations such as Church World Service (CWS), the US Conference of Catholic Bishops, and the Hebrew Immigrant Aid Society also have their origins in the 1940s post-war resettlement surge. Even at a time when the United States was concerned with post–Depression era unemployment and when anti-Semitism was clearly present, Americans in churches assisted arriving refugees locally and by supporting their particular denomination's refugee assistance organizations.

Dean Neher currently sits on the Refugee Resettlement Committee at Bridgewater Church of the Brethren in Bridgewater, Virginia. The congregation has been involved in refugee resettlement for more than fifty years, working with other churches to help settle refugees from sixteen countries.[9] Neher himself has been doing this work even longer, including serving as a church volunteer in both Germany and Greece after World War II.[10] He recalls that in the face of the overwhelming need, combined with lack of resources, the church didn't hesitate to step in and offer aid. "There was a need and awareness that something needed to be done. The war was over, and we'd get things to improve," he says. In the face of what might have been seen as a desperate and even hopeless situation, Neher notes, "There was a sense of optimism."

Back in the United States, much of the post-war effort centered on the East Coast, where refugees arrived by ship to begin the long, arduous process of resettlement. Yet, churches across the country banded together in other ways to meet the needs of displaced people worldwide. In 1947, with severe food shortages in Europe and a successful harvest season in the US, churches organized what became known as the Friendship Train, which traveled across the wheat belt collecting surplus food to be shipped overseas. In the words of journalist Drew Person, this aid came from "every dinner table in America," with the church often providing the infrastructure to collect and distribute it.[11] Packages of relief aid were labeled with the words: "All races and creeds make up the vast melting pot of America, and in a democratic and Christian spirit of good will toward men, we, the American people, have worked together to bring this food to your doorsteps."[12] Even with governments contributing post-war relief, churches and community members recognized a need and acted to fill it.

"MAN'S DISORDER"

To some degree, the ability to respond in the face of such a daunting crisis may be connected to the willingness of people and churches to work together, giving rise to an ecumenical and interfaith collaboration in the 1930s and '40s that is still the hallmark of refugee assistance today. For example, the Federal Council of Churches (FCC), a Protestant collaborative organization, turned its attention to the refugee crisis, beginning with a 1937 appeal on behalf of German Christian refugees. Its bulletin called for "an outpouring of Christ-like sympathy for no other reason than that men are in need."[13] As further evidence of this cross-collaboration, the FCC worked with the YMCA, the YWCA, the American Bible Society, the World Student Christian Federation, and the American Friends Service Committee as the Church Committee for Overseas Relief and Reconstruction.[14] The World Council of Churches, today a collaborative organization of over 300 global, national, and local church bodies, convened its first assembly in 1948 under the theme "Man's Disorder and God's Design."

"Man's disorder" has challenged the church with several massive refugee crises since World War II that are not as familiar in our country's memory. For example, when India was partitioned into Muslim-majority Pakistan and Hindu-majority India in 1947, 14 million people poured over borders according to their religious distinctions. Due to the immediacy and massive numbers of the migration, issues of hunger, disease, and lack of shelter were acute. One Presbyterian missionary reported that "hundreds of thousands of people were sitting . . . out in the open, huddled in groups."[15] US churches sent an immediate $70,000 in medical supplies, followed by $100,000 worth of famine relief via CWS.[16] Methodist schools in the area became refugee relief centers.[17] Additional aid from US churches provided "milk bars" along roads in key locations, where refugees could find food and other sustenance as they traveled.

Other massive global refugee crises include migration after the 1971 war in Bangladesh (10 million displaced) and the 1979 Soviet invasion of Afghanistan (6.3 million displaced). In each case, the largest providers of aid overall were the receiving communities, host governments, and international aid organizations. However, US churches also responded, often filling significant gaps in needed relief and development.

The church's history of response is woven through other major events in the past seventy-five years as well. Turning the focus closer to home, large groups of Cubans migrated to the United States after the 1959 revolution in their country. Many of these refugees are among the over 1.3 million Cubans living in the US today as contributing community members.[18] As the number of Cuban refugees joining family, friends, and the workforce in Miami peaked, available resources were saturated. Between 1962 and 1963, sixty-three flights from Miami transported over 3,000 individuals to thirty-five cities across the country where congregations and communities had agreed to welcome them. In 1980, CWS played a central role in responding to the more than 100,000 Cubans arriving as part of the Mariel Boatlift.

Though the American church wrestled with the divisive politics around the Vietnam War, it rose above the discord and provided assistance on many fronts to the people displaced by the conflict. In 1967, in a letter to the US Senate, the director of CWS spoke of the ecumenical efforts in Vietnam as "not primarily a material aid or feeding program; it is a program of Christians serving alongside refugees in desperate need in order to help as constructively as we may."[19] The World Council of Churches launched a $5 million program in Southeast Asia.[20] More than 100,000 Southeast Asian refugees were resettled in the United States in 1975,[21] many assisted and welcomed by local churches in partnership with local resettlement agencies.

In the broadest sense, the American church was involved in refugee resettlement long before the US had immigration laws, indeed long before there was a United States at all. By 1630, some 20,000 Puritans had emigrated to North America from England seeking religious freedom.[22] The influx of people leaving their homelands under desperate circumstances and coming to what became the United States continued for hundreds of years. By the early 1900s, for example, more than 100,000 Swedish people were living in Chicago. These immigrants, some of whom were refugees, relied on churches such as Chicago's St. Ansgarius Episcopal Church, Immanuel Lutheran Church, and First Swedish Methodist Episcopal Church for resources and resettlement assistance. The local church eased the transition of refugees to life in Chicago by assisting newcomers with finding jobs, social support, and housing.[23]

This brief history doesn't begin to cover the full scope of the church's response to refugees, especially over the past seventy-five years. And it shouldn't be seen as promoting the work of the church over and above the essential role of governments, local communities, and other international bodies, which are, in many cases, the more logical and effective sources of aid and relief. Nor is this focus on church action meant to raise the value of charitable acts above the ultimate need for worldwide human rights, peace, and justice. To further temper the optimism here, even within the study of church history, plenty of church publications and leaders have been unwilling to acknowledge the needs of displaced people, and some refugee assistance campaigns have fallen far short of their goals. That said, it remains true that targeted, successful responses to crises of displacement are part of the church's history and understanding of its mission in a broken world.

FILLING THE GAPS

While the church's work with refugees has been an important expression of God's love and care, it's also the case that the work of the church— specifically the work of Christian non-governmental organizations (NGOs)— continues to play a crucial role in global relief and development. Between 1994 and 2003, the UNHCR channeled over $721 million to faith-based organizations. William Headley, of Catholic Relief Services, reports that one third of all AIDS patients in the world are served through the Catholic Church.[24] In addition to these efforts quantified by organizational budgets, there are many smaller churches and NGOs whose impact is not as well publicized or well funded.

For a variety of reasons, Christian NGOs are well situated to deliver aid to people displaced by conflict: Many countries, including the US, trace the origins of their earliest schools and hospitals to the work of Christian missionaries. These education and health care networks offer well-established logistical infrastructures in areas of conflict.[25] Clergy and church communities serve as communication networks, often providing initial information at the onset of a crisis. In Sudan, for example, clergy initially communicated the impending human rights crisis, long before the media or international NGOs were paying attention. Churches are also well situated to sustain aid and development in dangerous or threatening circumstances. When international NGOs evacuated staff from Iraq due to security concerns, the Middle East Council of Churches, with networks of Iraqis, remained an acting partner for World Council of Churches assistance.[26] In the same way, church networks often remain in a community post-conflict, providing sustainable and ongoing relief and development.

These local church networks and other Christian NGOs are often well established in the places displaced persons live. Perhaps contrary to conventional belief, the majority of refugees live in urban areas, not refugee camps, and several Christian NGOs have programs addressing this reality. The Catholic organization Jesuit Refugee Service operates an urban refugee program in Kenya. CWS launched pilot programs in Rwanda, South Africa, and Tanzania, connecting urban refugees to job opportunities.[27] Many local churches also meet the critical needs of urban refugees; St. Andrew's United Church of Cairo in Egypt is just one example. In 1979, St. Andrew's began serving refugees and asylum seekers from current-day Ethiopia, Eritrea, Iraq, South Sudan, Sudan, and Somalia. They support a broad array of programs, including education, professional development opportunities, legal assistance, and psychosocial services.

A former St. Andrew's staff person explains that some refugees in the area aren't able to access UNHCR or other services safely.[28] She told me about a man from Eritrea who had been abducted by human traffickers who kidnap and torture their captives, seeking to extort a ransom from their desperate families. Though now out of captivity, he was living in fear and isolation in Cairo. St. Andrew's helped him complete an application for refugee status with hopes of resettlement in a third country. This is one of the many examples of churches addressing a unique gap in the services UNHCR or government programs can provide to urban refugees.

Christian organizations are also active in improving conditions for people living in refugee camps, often coordinating efforts to provide a wide range of services. For example, more than 270,000 people live in the Dadaab camp in Kenya—roughly the population of Orlando. The Lutheran World Federation provides elementary-level education, early childhood education, and support for older adults and individuals with disabilities.[29] World Vision provides food. CWS operates the Resettlement Support Center, which reviews the cases of Dadaab residents referred for resettlement, as well as providing cultural orientation for those accepted for resettlement in the US.

While NGOs and government agencies work together to provide essential services within refugee camps, there is also a recognition that refugees themselves bring skills and support systems that can fill in the gaps, even as they cope with significant loss and trauma. I spoke with a thirty-three-year-old Maryland resident who spent his childhood in the UmRakuba refugee camp in eastern Sudan. He told me that families built their own homes, maintained gardens, and purchased and sold dairy and other products. "People helped each other," he explained. "This was not a situation of plenty; all of this is happening in a place of not having. Displacement makes you come together if you are going to make it." The Orthodox church within the camp served as a great support to refugees. "Church," he said, "was a huge part of our community and way of life. It permeated daily living." While some food assistance came from the UNHCR and Christian organizations other than his own Orthodox community, the bulk of his family's food came from their own garden and the money his mother sent from her job in Khartoum.[30]

A BORDERLESS FAITH

Churches and Christian NGOs have one other important distinction that makes them well suited for refugee assistance: their work is bound only by their belief in the inherent value of every person created by God. Although there is an international framework for human rights and protections, these rights and securities are managed by governments. Each nation interprets and enforces international law through its own cultural lens and state rule. But refugees are stateless. They are not citizens of the places they live and often fall outside the protections afforded to citizens. The Christian faith is borderless and grounded in belief in the inherent value of people because, regardless of nationality, they are made in the image and likeness of God. In other words, faith-based NGOs fill an important gap in a world where powerful states value people based on citizenship.

Since 1975, more than 3 million refugees have resettled in the US after being accepted by the US State Department.[31] All arriving refugees begin their new life here with support from the State Department's US Refugee

Admissions Program (USRAP). They access professional case management and job development services through the USRAP's reception and placement program. However, in the words of Lutheran Immigration and Refugee Services, "Governments do not integrate newcomers, people do."[32] In the US, such people, often as part of a church, have been welcoming their neighbors in one of the most remarkable examples we have of ecumenical, interfaith, local, national, and international collaboration.

I spoke with a woman living in Chapel Hill, North Carolina, who is a member of the Karen ethnic minority of southern and eastern Myanmar. She escaped persecution there and came to the United States as a refugee.[33] She arrived through the USRAP, but it was a local church that provided her with furniture and necessities. She describes how church members took her to health appointments and job interviews in her critical first months here, allowing her to integrate into the community more quickly than if she'd had to navigate a new city alone. But beyond the practical help, the kindness of church members made her feel like she had family and friends in her new community. Today, she works as an interpreter for a community organization, her husband is on staff at a local hotel, and their three children are in school. They are members of a local church of refugees from Myanmar who welcome other newly arrived families with logistical and social support.

Back at Dean Neher's church, Bridgewater Church of the Brethren, its pastor, Chris Zepp, sees involvement with refugee resettlement as a way for the congregation to "invest resources of self and community."[34] Since welcoming their first refugee family in 1957, Bridgewater has assisted newcomers from Cuba, Russia, Eritrea, Ethiopia, Vietnam, and other areas of conflict or persecution. Most recently, the church welcomed a family from Syria. When a new family arrives, the whole congregation pitches in to contribute furniture, food, and household items. A smaller group of members gives of their time assisting with appointments and helping the family get integrated into the life of the community. Bridgewater and neighboring Harrisonburg aren't big cities with lots of resources. Nor is the church particularly large or affluent. However, they have welcomed more than 300 refugees over the last fifty years. This local church has stepped in at the community level to fill the gaps around the work of government agencies and NGOs.

THE BIBLICAL BASIS FOR REFUGEE RESPONSE

Human history is a narrative of disruption and migration, and that history is our history. Look around the room at any gathering. Most of us are just a few generations removed from a story of displacement. Some of our families came to this country seeking economic opportunity, some came unwillingly and violently through the global slave trade, and others came seeking religious freedom. Still others were forced from their native lands by the government. Refugees are not living some strange and foreign existence. That they have crossed borders and escaped persecution puts them squarely in the same human story as every person reading this book.

This human story is clearly on display in the Bible. Over and over, the biblical narrative tells of people on the move in a world plagued with human conflict. Rev. Joan Maruskin refers to the Bible as "The Ultimate Immigration Handbook." It's not hard to see why. The Bible, she writes, "begins with the migration of God's Spirit and ends with John in exile on the Isle of Patmos."[35] In between are the stories of Noah, Abraham, Sarah, Isaac, Jacob, Moses and the Israelites, Ezekiel, Isaiah, Naomi, Ruth, Esther, Mary, Joseph, Jesus—all of them migrants who left their homelands due to economic need, natural disaster, or persecution. The Bible asks us to remember our not-so-distant connection to those without a home, to "remember that you were a slave in the land of Egypt, and the Lord your God redeemed you" (Deuteronomy 15:15).

Still, it's not enough to acknowledge the commonality of our stories. The Bible also compels us to respond to refugees and to care for them. The book of Leviticus cuts right to the chase: "The alien who resides with you shall be to you as the citizen among you; you shall love the alien as yourself, for you were aliens in the land of Egypt: I am the Lord your God" (Leviticus 19:34). The message of caring for the needy—specifically those escaping oppression and violence—is not limited to a few passages. Theologian Orlando Espín says that welcoming the stranger is the most often-repeated command in the Hebrew Scriptures, second only to the command to worship God.[36] The Bible even anticipates the fear and desire for self-preservation that often keep us from extending a welcome to those in need:

> If there is among you anyone in need, a member of your community in any of your towns within the land that the Lord your God is giving you, do not be hard-hearted or tight-fisted toward your needy neighbor. You

should rather open your hand, willingly lending enough to meet the need, whatever it may be. Be careful that you do not entertain a mean thought, thinking, "The seventh year, the year of remission, is near," and therefore view your needy neighbor with hostility and give nothing; your neighbor might cry to the Lord against you, and you would incur guilt. Give liberally and be ungrudging when you do so, for on this account the Lord your God will bless you in all your work and in all that you undertake. Since there will never cease to be some in need on the earth, I therefore command you, "Open your hand to the poor and needy neighbor in your land" (Deuteronomy 15:7-11).

We also find this command woven into the New Testament, where Jesus is often shown in the role of stranger, guest, or host. He is a stranger who is provided dinner and hospitality by two disciples he approached on the road to Emmaus (Luke 24:13-35). He is a guest in the home of Mary, Martha, and Lazarus (Luke 10:38-42). He is a host, preparing room for us in the Father's house (John 14:2-3). It's easy to interpret the hospitality demonstrated in these passages (and many others) through our modern lens—warmly welcoming friends and family, maybe even someone from our own community whom we've never met. But hospitality in the ancient world involved a significant level of challenge and discomfort. Travelers didn't have the option of hotels and restaurants; they relied on individual households to take them in and offer food and shelter without regard for who they were, where they were from, or why they were traveling. There was an inherent risk in welcoming a literal stranger into your home, but hospitality meant doing it anyway. On this, Jesus was clear:

> Then the king will say to those at his right hand, "Come, you that are blessed by my Father, inherit the kingdom prepared for you from the foundation of the world; for I was hungry and you gave me food, I was thirsty and you gave me something to drink, I was a stranger and you welcomed me, I was naked and you gave me clothing, I was sick and you took care of me, I was in prison and you visited me." Then the righteous will answer him, "Lord, when was it that we saw you hungry and gave you food, or thirsty and gave you something to drink? And when was it that we saw you a stranger and welcomed you, or naked and gave you clothing? And when was it that we saw you sick or in prison and visited you?" And the king will answer them, "Truly I tell you, just as you did it to one of the least of these who are members of my family, you did it to me" (Matthew 25:34-40).

Inherent in the Christian faith is a belief in the value of each person, regardless of status, nationality, or legal standing. We aren't asked to discount these factors, but Jesus tells us that they aren't the whole story. He asks us to see the whole person, a person created and loved by God.

As individuals, as neighbors, and as members of communities of faith, we are a crucial part of the discussion and response to the current refugee crisis. Although we might not personally know a refugee from Afghanistan or be able to outline the timeline of the war in Syria, we have inherited a long history of involvement in the lives of refugees. For generations, the global church has mobilized resources and partnered with governments and other organizations to aid displaced people. While modern infrastructure has made some previous responses obsolete—think the Friendship Train—it remains the case that the church can respond to large humanitarian needs and does so effectively. As Christ-followers living in a world with so many displaced, it is our privilege to continue this work.

With a career spanning the local, state, and national level, Brianne Casey has had a front-row view of Christ followers, faith communities, and refugees creating stronger, more vibrant communities. Brianne facilitated local church engagement for Lutheran Services Carolinas, most recently serving as national community and ecumenical engagement coordinator for Church World Service in New York, NY. She holds a BA in ESL education from James Madison University and a MA in community development and planning from Clark University.

ENDNOTES

1   Bob Smietana, "Churches twice as likely to fear refugees than to help them," LifeWay Newsroom, February 29, 2016, https://blog.lifeway.com/newsroom/2016/02/29/churches-twice-as-likely-to-fear-refugees-than-t%C2%AD%C2%AD%C2%ADo-help-them/.

2   United Nations High Commissioner for Refugees (UNHCR), "The State of the World's Refugees 2000: Fifty Years of Humanitarian Action," January 1, 2000, http://www.unhcr.org/4a4c754a9.html.

3   United States Holocaust Museum. Holocaust Encyclopedia: Kristallnacht. Retrieved February 11, 2018, from www.ushmm.org/wlc/en/article.php?ModuleId=10005201.

4   William E. Nawyn, *American Protestantism's Response to Germany's Jews and Refugees: 1933-1941 (Studies in American history and culture)* (Ann Arbor: UMI Research Press, 1981), 30:65.

5   Nawyn, 41.

6   Ronald E. Stenning, *Church World Service: Fifty Years of Help and Hope* (New York: Friendship Press, 1996).

7   Peyton G. Craighill, "The Ministry of The Episcopal Church In The United States of America to Immigrants And Refugees: A Historical Outline," *Historical Magazine of the Protestant Episcopal Church* 51, no. 2 (June 1982): 203-218.

8   "Lutheran Immigration and Refugee Service History," Lutheran Immigration and Refugee Services, accessed April 29, 2018, https://www.lirs.org/our-work/about-us/historyfaith/.

9   "Refugee Resettlement: Bridgewater Church of the Brethren's Hospitality House," Bridgewater Church of the Brethren, accessed April 29, 2018, http://bwcob.org/mission/refugee-resettlement/.

10   Dean Neher, phone interview, December 22, 2017.

11   Stenning, 45.

12   "The 1947 Friendship Food Train to Europe," The Friendship Train of 1947, accessed February 11, 2018, http://thefriendshiptrain1947.org/.

13   Nawyn, 61.

14   Stenning, 45.

15   David S., "Dispatches from Partition," *Presbyterian Historical Society Blog* (blog), Presbyterian Historical Society, December 2, 2014, https://www.history.pcusa.org/blog/2014/12/dispatches-partition.

16   David S.

17   Rajni S. Mann, "The Methodist High Schools and Boys' Home in Sonipat," *New World Outlook: The Mission Magazine of the United Methodist Church*, May/June 2005: 18-19.

18   Jeanne Batalova and Jie Zong, "Cuban Immigrants in the United States," *Migration Information Source*, November 9, 2017, http://www.migrationpolicy.org/article/cuban-immigrants-united-states.

19   James MacCracken, "Statement Before the Senate Subcommittee to Investigate Problems Connected with Refugees and Escapees of the Senate Committee on the Judiciary," The Goshen Plowshares Collection, Oct. 4, 1967, http://replica.palni.edu/cdm/compoundobject/collection/gopplow/id/10223/rec/1.

20   Christe R. House, "75 Years with UMCOR," *New World Outlook: The Mission Magazine of the United Methodist Church*, January/February 2015: 22.

21   Jeanne Batalova and Jie Zong, "Vietnamese Immigrants in the United States," *Migration Information Source*, June 8, 2016, http://www.migrationpolicy.org/article/vietnamese-immigrants-united-states.

22   "Religion and the Founding of the American Republic," The Library of Congress, accessed December 21, 2017, http://www.loc.gov/exhibits/religion/rel01.html.

23   Anita Olson Gustafson, "Swedes," *Encyclopedia of Chicago*, accessed December 21, 2017, http://www.encyclopedia.chicagohistory.org/pages/1222.html.

24   Elizabeth Ferris, "Faith and Humanitarianism: It's Complicated," Journal of Refugee Studies 24, no. 3 (September 2011): 606-625.

25   Ferris, 606-625.

26   Elizabeth Ferris, "Faith based and secular humanitarian organizations," *International Review of the Red Cross* 87, no. 858 (June 2005): 311-325.

27   *Urban Refugee Self-Reliance Pilot Program in Rwanda, South Africa and Tanzania*, Church World Service, http://cwsglobal.org/wp-content/uploads/2016/02/urban-self-reliance-report-revised-2016-02-02.pdf.

28   Anonymous email interview, December 13, 2017.

29   "Kenya-Djibouti," Lutheran World, accessed February 9, 2017, https://www.lutheranworld.org/content/kenya-djibouti.

30   Anonymous phone interview, December 27, 2017.

31   "Refugee Admissions," Bureau of Population, Refugees, and Migration, accessed December 21, 2017, https://www.state.gov/j/prm/ra/.

32   *The Real Cost of Welcome: A Financial Analysis of Local Refugee Reception* (Baltimore, MD: Lutheran Immigration and Refugee Service, 2009).

33   Anonymous phone interview, 2017.

34   Chris Zepp, phone interview, December 22, 2017.

35   Rev. Joan M. Maruskin, "The Bible as the Ultimate Immigration Handbook: Written by, for, and about migrants, immigrants, refugees, and asylum seekers," CWS Immigration and Refugee Program, https://www.greatplainsumc.org/files/ministries/mj_bible_immigration_handbook.pdf.

36   Orlando O. Espín, "Immigration and Theology: Reflections by an Implicated Theologian," *Perspectivas: Occasional Papers (Hispanic Theological Initiative)*, no. 10 (Fall 2006): 46-47.

2

A PEOPLE WITHOUT A PLACE

THE GLOBAL MIGRATION CRISIS

BY DR. BETH OPPENHEIM-CHAN

In 2017, the world set a new record. According to the World Economic Forum, one in every 113 people in the world is now a refugee. Someone is displaced from their home by violence, war, or persecution every three seconds.[1] People around the globe leave their countries of origin for a variety of reasons. In the noise of our daily news feeds, it's sometimes hard to sort through what those reasons are and why they matter. Run a simple search on "migration" in the *New York Times*, for example, and you'll find hundreds of articles discussing the topic, each telling a unique story about the hows and whys of a particular migration pattern. Some movement is due to climate change,[2] some to conflict,[3] and some to reasons yet to be determined. As we consider how best to address the current refugee crisis, it helps to get some sense of the multiple causes, populations, and responses to human displacement.

In 2015, the United Nations released a report titled "Trends in International Migration: The 2015 Revision," which looked at all the ways people—some of whom are refugees and some of whom are not—around the globe move. It provided an interesting snapshot of just how many different types of populations move. The report shows that the number of international migrants has grown faster than the world's population—in 2015 there were 224 million people living in a country other than the one in which they were born, almost 20 million of whom were refugees. And while many of these people move far from their birthplace, most migration happens between countries in the same part of the world. The report also shows that two-thirds of all international migrants live in just twenty countries.[4] This data gives us a glimpse of the inherent diversity in displacement—it's never about one group of people moving to one new place to escape one problem. The complexity of international migration requires a complex international strategy to ensure the safety and well-being of those who find themselves on the move, whether by choice or by force.

WHO ARE REFUGEES?

The nature of the current national debate about refugees might lead some to believe this is a fairly modern phenomenon. However, the reality is that most contemporary infrastructure around refugees and other displaced people came into effect in the post–World War II era. At the forefront of these efforts are a wide variety of players: non-governmental organisations (NGOs), policymakers (local and national governments), the United Nations, and the people themselves.

In 1950, the office of the United Nations High Commissioner for Refugees (UNHCR) was created to assist with the mass migration underway as displaced people tried to make their way either home or abroad after the war in Europe. Today, UNHCR remains one of the critical agencies involved in the regulation of the movement of displaced people across the globe.

The most well-known piece of global legislation on displacement, the 1951 Refugee Convention,[5] helped codify the definition of *refugee* in an effort to recognize such people as a distinct subset of migrant populations. The new definition outlined the legal obligations of nation-states to protect refugees. This legal instrument remains the measuring tool of the UNHCR to declare displaced persons as refugees, as opposed to other types of migrants. The Convention defines a refugee as:

> A person who, owing to a well-founded fear of being persecuted for reasons of race, religion, nationality, membership of a particular social group or political opinion, is outside the country of his nationality and is unable or, owing to such fear, is unwilling to avail himself of the

protection of that country; or who, not having a nationality and being outside the country of his former habitual residence as result of such events, is unable or, owing to such fear, is unwilling to return to it.[6]

This definition legally separated refugees seeking asylum from the broader category of migrants, and subsequently created a framework for figuring out how to allow for the movement of refugees from around the world. In a post-war context, the need for legal protection for people who seemed to have no state to go back to was even more prescient. It defined not only those seeking to escape persecution, but also the mechanisms through which they could seek rights-based protection in new countries. Today, we use the term *refugee* to refer to anyone in the world who meets the standard laid out in the 1951 Convention. UNHCR is the only agency worldwide with the legal authority to designate someone a refugee and issue the appropriate documentation.

Asylees, while related to refugee status, are slightly different. Refugees can be designated anywhere around the globe. They may be in a country where they'd like to remain, or in a country near their home country where they are awaiting a more permanent status. Asylees have, through their own means, travelled to a country where they would like to remain and seek asylum. Already *being* in the physical country where they would like to stay is what makes asylees different from a refugee, at least from a definition standpoint.

For example, a Somali refugee in a refugee camp in Kenya is considered a refugee once they have been screened by UNHCR and given the proper documentation. They are now eligible to seek potential protection as a refugee either in Kenya or in another country. An asylee is that same Somali who has travelled on their own to the United States and arrives at the border seeking asylum. They have made it to the country where they would like to remain and are declaring their intent at a border crossing.[7]

Finally, immigrants, sometimes referred to simply as migrants, are people who travel to a country outside of their country of origin but do not meet the criteria laid out under the 1951 Convention. Simply seeking better economic conditions is not enough to qualify someone as a refugee, and therefore this person would be designated an immigrant or an economic migrant.

While somewhat technical, this terminology is important—both for people interested in helping refugees and immigrants and for policymakers. Today, we hear a great deal about refugees and the conditions that led them to flee their homes to find a better life. It's incredibly important to continue to understand the difference between refugee stories and stories of migration, and to understand the ways in which they both contribute to the narrative around global movement.

THE SCREENING PROCESS

In determining and managing those with refugee status, the role of the UNHCR is paramount. The process for this is known as Refugee Status Determination, or RSD.[8] As noted in their 2013 report, the UNHCR carries out this work in many locations across the globe. This was the case even prior to the Syrian civil war and the influx of Syrian refugees to Europe and elsewhere.

The process is comprehensive, and while it varies slightly depending on the context, it is constantly being evaluated to ensure fairness for every population who needs it. There are specifics in place for RSD that have to do with the types of claims being made (sexual violence, political persecution, etc.), but the determination process remains exhaustive and can be made more complex depending upon the circumstances.

The RSD process involves interviews, document searches, and the development of a comprehensive narrative of "flight." This allows the UN to build a picture of that person's life, their family history, and the ways in which their situation fits into the definition of *refugee*. Of the many thousands of people screened each year for refugee status, fewer than 5 percent are recommended for resettlement.

One of the easiest ways to understand this complex process is to think about inclusion and exclusion. Let's take the example of a Burundian individual seeking refuge in Kenya. He is granted an interview by UNHCR and is screened first for *inclusion* in the refugee definition, as laid out by the 1951 Convention. He describes fleeing Burundi because he feared for his safety as a member of the opposition political party in the country. He has arrived in Kenya and is seeking refugee documents to remain in Kenya. Additionally, the UN scans for *exclusion*; that is, if he is deemed a refugee because of how and why he fled his country, what might exclude him from seeking protection formally? Such factors might include being a high-ranking military or police official, or having other criminal activity on his record. If he is not deemed to be excluded, he is given refugee status and the protection it affords under the 1951 Convention.

Needless to say, this process is very personal. The impact of telling and retelling horrific experiences of trauma is one that many refugees have indicated as triggering post-traumatic stress disorder. It also sheds light on the ways in which having family members still in harm's way impacts the daily life of refugees worldwide.[9] During interviews, refugees often express concern about the speed with which family members can join them in the United States. Family reunification remains a lengthy process, fraught with its own complexities and policy challenges.

FROM SCREENING TO RESETTLEMENT

UNHCR estimates that it takes two years for refugees to move from the initial resettlement screening to being resettled in the US. Family reunification cases often take much longer; families might wait three years or more from the time the application is filed until the family is reunited. Process times may vary based on the kind of reunification the family is eligible for, their nationality and location, the required security checks for that population, and when staff are available to conduct interviews in their location.

Furthermore, the expiration of security and medical checks due to delays in interview cycles can further delay cases, as can any discrepancies in information that need to be resolved before the case can proceed. Such discrepancies can be as small as the way a name is spelled or a year of birth—in countries that don't keep consistent birth records, these are incredibly difficult to maintain. Discrepancies in UNHCR registration documents can also affect the case. This assumes the case is even accepted for resettlement. Many families wait years, only to have the US Department of Homeland Security determine that their case does not meet grounds for persecution based on the UN refugee definition, or for the president to change the number of refugees the US will admit for the year. Even a short-term hold on resettlement from certain countries can push refugees from those countries back into the process if any of their documentation expires during that time. The highly regulated RSD screening process seeks to marry the need for safety and security for those who have experienced traumatic, life-altering circumstances with the legal framework designed to protect host nations and their populations.

The process a refugee goes through is only part of the overall picture of resettlement. Host nations are a critical piece of the refugee's journey. Whether it's the country of first asylum for a refugee or the country where the refugee hopes to settle permanently, the host country plays a large role in shaping the experience of displacement and resettlement. One particularly interesting example of this is the country of Kenya. Because of its geographic location, Kenya has played host to refugees and displaced people from across the region, including Somalis, Sudanese and South Sudanese, Ethiopians, and Congolese people. Kenya is also home to the largest refugee camp in the world, Dadaab, which is home to a quarter of a million people. Additionally, refugees live in urban areas throughout Kenya, which means the number of refugees in-country is much higher.[10]

More recently, refugee camps in Europe have hosted refugees fleeing conflict in Syria and other Middle Eastern countries, as well as North Africa. The year 2015 saw a large wave of refugees from Syria cross land and sea into mainland Europe. It is believed that more than one million people made the dangerous crossing, attempting to reach safety as the Syrian civil war raged.[11] This placed Europe back at the forefront of the displacement crisis, forcing these countries to have discussions and debates about just how much responsibility—both financial and logistical—they bear for displaced people fleeing conflict and oppression in other parts of the world.

Many Syrian refugees entered the continent through some of its poorest countries, such as Greece and Macedonia. Since the initial influx, the European Union has taken steps to close some of its borders to refugees, forcing them to travel more challenging routes to gain access to safety. This has also led to even more Syrian refugees fleeing into neighbouring countries such as Lebanon and Jordan, both of which are already hosting numbers of refugees that far surpass those in Europe.[12] While this is a different context than some of the African and Asian countries hosting refugees, it is indicative of the global reality: as long as the root causes of displacement remain, pipelines of people attempting to get to safety will continue to exist.

THE POLITICS OF ACCEPTANCE

Since the 1951 Convention was enacted, many global conflicts have contributed to an increase in the number of people seeking refuge worldwide. These have included but are not limited to political conflict and crises in countries such as Myanmar,[13] Rwanda, the Democratic Republic of Congo, Cambodia, Iraq, Afghanistan, and, most recently, Syria. There is every reason to believe this uptick will continue, which means international humanitarian policy remains critical for creating a baseline of assistance for those who need it.

When people begin fleeing a particular geographic area or country, there is need for an immediate response. This is usually in the form of emergency shelter and food and water provisions. While there is little debate about the need for safety and protection for these vulnerable individuals, the debate still rages about the best way to bring that about. How can countries—particularly low-income countries—adequately provide for both their own citizens and those who are fleeing conflict or other displacement situations?

Many countries around the world have decided to host refugees in camps, adhering to what is referred to as encampment policy. The policy simply means that if refugees are registered in-country as refugees, they must reside in camps while awaiting a more permanent solution such as resettlement to a third country. Some argue that this makes it easier for NGOs and host governments to provide services to the population, such as housing, food, and health care.

While refugee camps undoubtedly provide opportunity for relative safety for those who are desperately fleeing conflict, they come with their own difficulties, which compound, the longer the refugee or refugee family is housed there. And many families are there for decades. Ben Rawlence's 2016 book, *City of Thorns: Nine Lives in the World's Largest Refugee Camp,* is a helpful resource for shedding light on the challenges of encampment policies.

Rawlence is one of many voices drawing attention to the fact that refugee camps are not about immediate safety but about a lack of a permanent solution. Nearly one-third of the people living in Dadaab refugee camp were *born* there.[14] The first, smaller camp in Dadaab was established in 1991, after Somali refugees began fleeing across the border into Kenya during their own civil war. Since then, the camp has grown to an estimated 235,269 registered refugees in 2016. Some people born in the camp have already reached their early twenties, stretching the legacy of Dadaab and the displacement complications it represents into another generation. Rawlence explains, "No one wants to admit that the temporary camp of Dadaab has become permanent: not the Kenyan government who must host it, not the UN who must pay for it, and not the refugees who must live there. This paradox makes the ground unsteady."[15]

These statistics are an indication of the protracted nature of this solution. They also tell us that, not only have temporary situations become permanent, but the international community has not yet found significant capacity to change this fact. Dadaab is not unique; as the Syrian crisis grows and refugees have fled north, camps have cropped up across the European continent.

This interpretation by Rawlence points to a critical challenge facing the refugee community as well as those who work to serve their needs. Permanent solutions to displacement come in several forms, none of which can happen in a vacuum. Coordination among nations, community organizations, and vast populations of people are all needed in order to figure out how to create solutions and make them sustainable.

While it's clear that many governments prefer a controlled environment where they can enforce boundaries for the refugees they are hosting, it's become a challenge to maintain this type of infrastructure as it becomes more apparent that displacement situations are likely to last for a long time. Consider the case of the Calais refugee camp in France, sometimes referred to as the "Jungle." Refugees fleeing places like Somalia and Eritrea began to gather here in the late 1990s in hopes of making their way to the United Kingdom. Eventually, it grew into an unofficial camp—more accurately, a set of camps around the region—despite the French government's continuous efforts to tear down structures and move people out. In 2015, there were efforts to create something more sustainable, but the permanence of some of the infrastructure being put in place by NGOs caused the French government to decide to tear the camp down for good in 2016.

The opposition to Calais provides a sort of microcosm of the issues surrounding displacement. Residents of the camp tell their stories in the book *Voices from the 'Jungle': Stories from the Calais Refugee Camp*, expressing the horror and abuse they experienced both in their home countries and in the camp, along with their disdain as the French government announced the destruction of the camp.[16] With the help of local grassroots organisations, residents of the camp had begun to create the bare necessities of a "normal" life as they awaited applications for resettlement in France, other European Union countries, the United Kingdom, or the United States. These included a football pitch, classrooms for education, vocational training, and access to computers. While this type of life speaks to the refugees' desire to retain normalcy and not stagnate in the face of desperate times, the opposite effect was felt by the French government, who saw permanence where they wanted swift resolution.

In many ways, the Calais refugee camp pitted local government against refugees.[17] Calais hosted many refugees who had family ties in the United Kingdom. They primarily used Calais as a temporary residence while waiting until the long UK security and vetting process was completed. This placed France in a complicated position: allow refugees to wait, with the hopes that they would ultimately be resettled elsewhere, or encourage them to apply for asylum in France itself. The French government, succumbing to pressure from right-wing conservatives in their own country as well as pressure from the United Kingdom, responded by tearing down the camp and forcing refugees to go elsewhere. While this did little if anything to address the root causes of displacement or concerns of either refugee or resident, the symbolic gesture spoke to a world where decisive action in times of tension is seen as better than serving humanitarian needs.

Politicians in Calais are not unique: political pressure is intense on the part of local populations to resolve issues of perceived security and health risks in places where refugees wait for resettlement. Some countries, most notably South Africa, have decided against encampment in any form. In South Africa, those seeking asylum must register with the government as a refugee and may live anywhere in the country thereafter.[18] Many times, host countries have populations of both: camps where refugees live for years awaiting a more permanent solution, and refugees who live in urban areas where they may have more access to work or family networks already there. Both are temporary solutions to a long-term problem.

Today, according to UNHCR, 2.6 million refugees live in camps globally. Host countries such as Ethiopia and Kenya harbour some of the largest camps despite also being low-income countries themselves. This is primarily due to geopolitical realities in the region. Consistent, ongoing conflict in countries such as Somalia and the Democratic Republic of Congo have resulted in a steady stream of people into the region's refugee camps.

The conversation about displacement and its effect on both refugees and host countries is ongoing, as are discussions about long-term solutions to the emergencies and conflicts that create refugees in the first place. Ultimately, the international community must come to agreement on solutions that will outlast current conflict, and help refugees achieve normalcy and sustainable protection.

THREE DURABLE SOLUTIONS

Solutions to displacement situations—particularly those situations that seem to have no end in sight—require what is referred to by the UN as "durable solutions."[19] This term refers to potential scenarios where those who have found themselves displaced can seek a more permanent residence where they can remain safe. While the term sounds optimistic, the number of durable solutions is limited. The three main solutions identified by the UN are voluntary repatriation, resettlement, and local integration. They reflect the fact that displacement is inherently messy and complex, and does not operate on official timetables.

While it would be easiest to say that one durable solution is preferable to another, it really depends on the context, the individual refugee's situation, and the evolving political situation in the country of origin. Regardless of the solution sought, making it happen requires a great deal of planning and decision making on the part of the refugee.

Voluntary repatriation

One of the least communicated realities about refugees is that the vast majority want to go home. Unlike immigrants or other types of migrants, refugees and asylum seekers have fled their countries of origin because they were forced to. Whether living in a camp or a city, refugees are quick to express that they miss where they came from. It's important to understand this, as it fundamentally shapes the way people perceive the end goals of refugees. Their end goal, by definition, is safety and security, but it's also a longing for home, for normalcy, for the intangible sense of belonging that comes from living where you want to live.

The UNHCR recognises the inherent complexity of repatriation and works directly with governments to mediate the realities felt on the ground when people return home after long periods of displacement. These can include competition for work, potential tensions between those who fled and those who remained, and reintegration into a society that has changed since the refugees left.

This has been true across country and continent contexts. According to UNHCR, the past two decades have seen 17.2 million people repatriated voluntarily.[20] However, they note that this rate has slowed in the past few years. While the conflicts that lead to displacement are often quite different, none of them are easy to recover from. Comprehensive voluntary repatriation must involve political and legislative action to ensure not just the physical movement of refugees but also their reintegration once they've returned home.

We can find examples of this solution working well in Afghanistan, Mozambique, and Myanmar. In all cases, robust cooperation between local governments and the UN allowed for repatriation that helped refugees re-adjust and gain access to critical services along the way. In Mozambique, refugees had fled to neighbouring countries and beyond after a long and bloody civil war in the mid-1990s. After the war, the government worked to bring people home again by offering incentives for voluntary repatriation, including land availability and deeds, employment assistance, and importing goods duty-free. Mozambique took these steps in partnership with the UN and the rest of the international community to ensure success at a particularly vulnerable time.

Local integration

Many refugees flee to neighbouring countries, technically known as countries of first asylum. These countries, as described in the above example of Kenya, may or may not be equipped for long-term hosting of displaced people. Some NGOs invest their resources in assisting these hosting nations, hoping to create better outcomes for refugees and hosts alike. For some western countries, supporting these initiatives is preferable to hosting refugees within their own borders.

For many refugee families, the decision to locally integrate into a country of first asylum is a pragmatic one, rather than a preferred one. While the high-unemployment conditions in Nairobi, for example, may not be as ideal for Somali families as those in, say, Minnesota, which has several growing and thriving Somali communities, it's important to keep in mind that Kenya borders Somalia—their home. In conversations with refugees in the predominantly Somali neighbourhood of Eastleigh in Nairobi, there are two refrains: one is to get to the United States or Europe, and the other is to get back to Somalia. In the meantime, refugees integrate into the community as best they can.

Local integration into these host countries is central to the success of this solution, for both the host community and the refugees themselves. A three-country research study conducted by the NGO Church World Service in 2012 analysed host community–refugee relations in Cameroon, Indonesia, and Pakistan. The findings were telling: Social networks, not traditional humanitarian services, were the primary source of support for refugees. The stronger the host community–refugee relations, the better the socioeconomic outcomes and protection outcomes for the refugees. Investment in local integration in the form of education, awareness, and vocational training will likely continue to be one of the more important durable solutions available to displaced people.

Resettlement

In talking about refugee and immigration policy, we most often think about the ramifications of the third durable solution, resettlement. In terms of numbers, the contrast between the attention resettlement receives and the data around it could not be starker. UNHCR lists more than 65.6 million people displaced globally, but only 189,300 refugees resettled in 2016. Debate rages in much of the western world over the acceptance of refugees, yet the percentage of those who actually gain access to the resettlement program of *any* developed country is exceptionally low.

In practice, resettlement is complicated. While the structure of resettlement programs varies from country to country, the United States has resettled the most refugees of any country worldwide. The resettlement program in the US and elsewhere is now under threat. Concerns connecting the resettlement of refugees to national security and the economy have posed a challenge not only for the refugees themselves but for the UNHCR, which operates under a system based on working with developed countries to fulfil their obligations under the 1951 Convention.

In 2017, the United States set the number of potentially acceptable refugees for resettlement at 45,000, the lowest number in the current resettlement program's history. While global displacement is at an all-time high, governments around the globe are changing their approach to resettlement as a durable solution and making it less and less accessible. The ramifications of this at the humanitarian level are clear: the less available resettlement becomes, the more likely it is that a new generation of refugees will be born and live out much of their lives in refugee camps in Kenya and elsewhere.

In the post–World War II era, displacement has continued to be a reality across the globe. While the causes of displacement vary, including climate change and natural disaster, conflict, discrimination, and persecution, the fact remains that migration, in all its forms, is not going away. Backed by a robust framework of international law, governance structures have operated in more or less the same way for decades, assuming a natural ebb and flow of people across the world between rich and poor countries. However, as conflict situations become more and more protracted, we find ourselves at a crossroads.

The United Nations and its refugee agency have helped negotiate with and among partners in the humanitarian infrastructure to define and sustain solutions for refugees and asylum seekers. The reality is that these solutions are multi-layered and complicated. A mirror image of the complexities that cause displacement in the first place, the durable solutions currently available to refugees are neither easily accessible nor guaranteed. Addressing these issues will continue to require willingness on the part of all nations to care for and ensure the safety of vulnerable people, no matter where they come from.

Dr. Beth Oppenheim-Chan is an international development specialist and researcher, currently working in the immigration and refugee space. She holds a master's degree in International Development & Humanitarian Assistance from New York University, and a PhD in Human Geography from the University of Cape Town, where the focus of her work was on identity and the intersection of responsibility and morality in Maputo, Mozambique. She is currently at work on a book on nonprofit organizations in the Global South, which will be published by Cambridge University Press.

ENDNOTES

1   Charlotte Edmond, "The Number of Displaced People in the World Just Hit a Record High," World Economic Forum, June 20, 2017, https://www.weforum.org/agenda/2017/06/there-are-now-more-refugees-than-the-entire-population-of-the-uk/.

2   Jessica Benko, "How a Warming Planet Drives Human Migration," *New York Times Magazine*, April 19, 2017, https://www.nytimes.com/2017/04/19/magazine/how-a-warming-planet-drives-human-migration.html.

3   Rod Nordland, "A Mass Migration Crisis, and It May Yet Get Worse," *The New York Times*, October 31, 2015, https://www.nytimes.com/2015/11/01/world/europe/a-mass-migration-crisis-and-it-may-yet-get-worse.html.

4   "224 Million International Migrants Living Abroad Worldwide, New UN Statistics Reveal," *Sustainable Development Goals,* The United Nations, accessed April 2018, http://www.un.org/sustainabledevelopment/blog/2016/01/244-million-international-migrants-living-abroad-worldwide-new-un-statistics-reveal/.

5   "The 1951 Refugee Convention," UNHCR, accessed April 2018, http://www.unhcr.org/afr/1951-refugee-convention.html.

6   "The 1951 Refugee Convention."

7   Department of Homeland Security, "Refugees & Asylum Seekers," U.S. Citizenship and Immigration Services, accessed April 2018, https://www.uscis.gov/humanitarian/refugees-asylum.

8   "Refugee Status Determination," The UN Refugee Agency, UNHCR, accessed April 2018, http://www.unhcr.org/refugee-status-determination.html.

9   UNHCR Regional Representation in Canberra, "Expert Roundtable on Mental Health in Refugee Status Determination," August 17, 2017, The UN Refugee Agency, UNHCR, http://www.unhcr.org/news/latest/2017/8/599540787/expert-roundtable-on-mental-health-in-refugee-status-determination.html.

10   "Kenya Registered Refugees and Asylum-seekers as of 31 December 2017," The UN Refugee Agency Infographic, UNHCR, December 2017, http://www.unhcr.org/ke/wp-content/uploads/sites/2/2018/01/Kenya-Statistics-Infographics_December-2017.pdf.

11   BBC, "Migrant Crisis: Migration to Europe Explained in Seven
      Charts," *BBC News*, March 4, 2016, http://www.bbc.com/news/
      world-europe-34131911.

12   Al Jazeera, "Refugees Found Frozen in Lebanon Near Syria Border,"
      News, Syrian Refugees, Al Jazeera, January 19, 2018, http://www.
      aljazeera.com/news/2018/01/refugees-frozen-lebanon-syria-bor-
      der-180119180011632.html.

13   The country name for Burma/Myanmar has wavered back and forth
      in the past several decades due to changes in political regime. At pres-
      ent, the country is called Myanmar.

14   Ian Bremmer, "These 5 Different Camps Tell the Story of the Global
      Refugee Crisis," *Time*, October 27, 2016, http://time.com/4547918/
      refugee-camps-calais-zaatari-dadaab-nakivale-mae-la/.

15   Ben Rawlence, *City of Thorns: Nine Lives in the World's Largest Refu-
      gee Camp* (New York: Picador, 2016), 201.

16   Marie Godin et al., eds., *Voices from the 'Jungle': Stories from the Calais
      Refugee Camp*, (London: Pluto Press, 2017).

17   Lucy Pasha-Robinson, "Mayor of Calais 'Bans Distribution of Food to
      Migrants,'" *The Independent*, March 2, 2017, http://www.independent.
      co.uk/news/world/europe/calais-mayor-natacha-bouchart-jungle-refu-
      gee-camp-ban-food-distribution-migrants-a7608676.html.

18   "Refugee Status & Asylum," Department of Home Affairs, Republic of
      South Africa, accessed April 2018, http://www.dha.gov.za/index.php/
      refugee-status-asylum.

19   UNHCR, "Durable Solutions," The UN Refugee Agency, UNHCR,
      accessed April 2018, http://www.unhcr.org/ke/durable-solutions.

20   "Executive Committee of the High Commissioner's Programme,"
      Standing Committee 66th meeting summary, meeting, June 7, 2016
      p, 3, http://www.unhcr.org/576ba6ec7.pdf.

3

A GLOBAL PERSPECTIVE

INTERNATIONAL POLICY AND THE ONGOING REFUGEE CRISIS

BY JENNY YANG

I spent my junior year of college studying abroad, in Madrid, Spain. I remember riding the subway along with an African woman and her young child when a group of rowdy Spanish teenagers boarded the train, took out cans of spray paint, and started spraying graffiti on the walls of the train. In Spanish, they wrote, "Get out of my country, black people." The teenagers got off the train at the next stop while I watched, astounded and angry. I went up to the young mother to see if she was okay, but she didn't want to talk. As I looked around to see how others were reacting, I was even more disturbed to see that no one else seemed bothered by what had happened.

Living in a country that has traditionally been a more homogeneous society than the United States, I started wondering what it must feel like for this young mom to see those words. I realized that true justice for her was about creating not just a more welcoming and affirming society, but a system of laws that would recognize her vulnerability and offer her legal protection, especially if she was fleeing persecution or danger. For this young mom, true flourishing required a culture of welcome. This experience opened my eyes to the local challenges of global forced migration and the long history of international efforts to respond.

In the aftermath of World War II, around 60 million people were forced to leave their homes. This included 12 million Germans who were displaced when Poland annexed large parts of Eastern Germany. It was the first time that an international body kept a record of such totals. It also prompted the world community to create a global governing body, the United Nations, which would in turn create the office of the United Nations High Commissioner for Refugees (UNHCR), tasked with facilitating a response to global displacement crises and creating global refugee policy.

THE 1951 CONVENTION AND THE 1967 PROTOCOL

The United Nations General Assembly adopted the statute that created the UNHCR on December 14, 1950. The 1951 Refugee Convention, ratified by 145 nation-states, defined the term *refugee* and outlined the rights of the displaced, as well as what nations are legally obligated to do to protect them: assist refugees with their most basic needs, including food and water, shelter, medical care, and education, and find durable solutions for refugees.[1] While the initial program was limited to those displaced within Europe before January 1, 1951, the 1967 Protocol removed the time limitations, making the Refugee Convention universally applicable. For years, the UNHCR had a temporary mandate that was renewed every five years, but in 2003, the United Nations General Assembly removed any time limit until such time as "the refugee problem is solved."[2]

The 1951 Convention and the 1967 Protocol establish the framework for the international response to the current displacement crisis, in which an estimated 65.6 million people are affected. Global displacement is presently at a record high, with distinct trends worth noting. For example, most of the world's displaced are not technically refugees because, though displaced from their homes, they still reside within the boundaries of their countries. In addition, half of the world's refugees come from just three countries: Syria, Afghanistan, and South Sudan. Roughly 84 percent of the world's refugees are hosted by developing countries, and about half the world's refugees are children. These dynamics mean that the international community will need to apply the instruments of international refugee law to unique contexts in order to promote the basic rights and dignity of displaced people, wherever they are.

At the center of global policy for displaced people is the 1951 Convention definition of a refugee as a person who, "owing to a well-founded fear of being persecuted for reasons of race, religion, nationality, membership in a particular social group, or political opinion, is outside the country of his or her nationality, and is unable to or, owing to such fear, is unwilling to avail himself of the protection of that country."[3] Countries often establish their own procedures to assess and register individuals as refugees within their borders but may rely on UNHCR's expertise to carry out such operations.

Nation-states are responsible for protecting their citizens, but when they are not able or willing to do so, and individuals flee to another country, the international community steps in—often through UNHCR—to ensure the protection and safety of those who might otherwise suffer serious human rights violations. Refugees are distinct within international migration law because they are forced to flee due to fear of persecution, as opposed to migrants who might leave their home country to seek greater opportunity or for family reunification purposes. As we look at global policy, it's important to keep in mind that people who voluntarily migrate often have the protection of their home country, whereas refugees often do not. This does not mean that migrants don't deserve the protection of the countries to which they have fled, but rather that a specific set of laws, principles, and policies is needed when dealing with those forced to flee due to persecution or fear of persecution.

The core principle of the 1951 Convention is *non-refoulement*, meaning that a refugee cannot or should not be returned to a country where there are serious threats to his or her life or freedom (Article 33). The principle of non-refoulement applies to all refugees as a customary part of international law; it is binding on all nation-states regardless of whether they ratified the 1951 Convention or the 1967 Protocol. The Convention also states other rights of refugees, including the right to freedom of movement in the territory (Article 26), the right to work (Articles 17 and 19), the right to housing (Article 21), the right to education (Article 22), the right to access the courts (Article 16), and the right to be issued identity and travel documents (Articles 27 and 28). These articles outline the safeguarding of a refugee's most basic human rights, including economic and social rights, ensuring that refugees living in a host country will be treated like the country's own citizens. The Convention's core principles and protections, however, do not apply to any person who has committed a crime against peace, a war crime, or a crime against humanity or who is guilty of acts contrary to the purposes and principles of the United Nations.

Despite the 1951 Convention and the 1967 Protocol, their principles are often ignored or violated due to national sovereignty or national security concerns. For example, while refugees are supposed to be afforded freedom of movement, an estimated 40 percent live in refugee camps and are often not able to leave.[4] Many refugees are not afforded the right to work and, as a result, may work in "underground" economies. In other cases, refugees cannot access medical care for urgent needs.

While the Convention established the principles of international refugee law, regional statutes also stipulate international obligations toward refugees and those living in refugee-like conditions. For example, in 1969, the Organization of African Unity (OAU) expanded the definition of *refugee* for its territories to include those fleeing a well-founded fear of persecution, as well as those who flee their place of habitual residence due to "external aggression, occupation, foreign domination or events seriously disturbing public order."[5] The OAU convention encourages member states to "secure the settlement of refugees" who are unable or unwilling to return home, and to grant temporary residence to such refugees.[6] The OAU convention also states that refugees who voluntarily repatriated to their home countries should not be penalized for such actions and should instead be given "every possible assistance" by their countries of both origin and asylum. The OAU convention was signed by forty-one heads of state in Africa.

The Cartagena Declaration on Refugees, Colloquium on the International Protection of Refugees in Central America, Mexico, and Panama was signed in 1984, incorporating the OAU's definition of a refugee and adding to it individuals who flee their country because "their lives, safety, or freedom have been threatened by generalized violence, foreign aggression, internal conflicts, massive violation of human rights or other circumstances which have seriously disturbed public order."[7] The Cartagena Declaration reaffirmed the principle of non-refoulement and the importance of family reunification as a fundamental principle in regard to refugees and the "peaceful, non-political and exclusively humanitarian nature" of the granting of asylum or refugee status.

These regional refugee statutes address specific humanitarian developments in the regions to which they pertain and reflect the obligation of nation-states to consider such political dynamics when granting refugee or asylum decisions to those entering their borders. These statutes have helped host countries adapt their laws and practices to specific scenarios such that those fleeing conflict and generalized violence can be afforded the same protections as those escaping more specific forms of persecution.

THREE DURABLE SOLUTIONS

The protections pursued by the UNHCR often fall into three categories of durable solutions for the displaced. You read briefly about these in the previous chapter, but it bears a closer look at the ways these solutions reflect global public policy and the need for international cooperation and support.

Voluntary repatriation

The preferable solution—and the desire for most refugees—is the ability to return home in safety and dignity. Many refugees stay in camps or urban settings for years, but when there is peace and safety in their home countries, they are often able to return. In 2016, 552,000 refugees returned to their home countries—double the number who did so in 2015, and the highest figure since 2008.[8] To enable the safe and secure return of refugees to their homes, there must be free and informed choice. This means that refugees cannot be forced to return home but must make the decision based on what they believe to be true about the political environment in their home country.

The key to successful voluntary repatriation is the facilitation of property and housing restitution, return assistance, and peace and reconciliation activities. One of the most significant and ongoing repatriations of refugees in the past few decades has been Afghans going back to Afghanistan. In the late 1970s, when the Soviet war began in Afghanistan, waves of Afghan refugees fled into Pakistan. Afghan refugees continued to arrive to Pakistan during Afghanistan's civil wars in the 1990s, and by 2001, there were four million Afghan refugees in Pakistan.[9] After the Taliban government was toppled in 2002, there was a large-scale repatriation of Afghan refugees and Internally Displaced Persons, mostly from Pakistan and Iran; this repatriation process continues today. From 2002 through 2016, 3.9 million Afghan refugees have voluntarily repatriated to Afghanistan, although 1.5 million still remain in Pakistan, constituting the largest ongoing refugee situation in the world.[10] The voluntary repatriation exercise of Afghan refugees was the largest in UNHCR's history as the agency provided transportation and cash assistance to returning refugees. The

Afghan Ministry for Rural Reconstruction and Development worked with international agencies like the United Nations Development Programme, the UN Food and Agriculture Organization, the World Food Program, and others to ensure that those who had been displaced had their basic needs met.

During the Burundian refugee repatriation in the mid-2000s, the issue of land was central to both the short-term and long-term success of reintegration. Because land-ownership rights were in dispute and there was significant overcrowding on farmed land, a system of compensation was necessary to provide returning refugees involved in land disputes with relocation aid or assistance in starting their own businesses.[11] World Relief, for example, partnered with the US Department of State to rebuild homes and provide livelihood activities for returning refugees. These activities were critical in order for refugees to have the physical and economic protections they needed alongside the legal protections the Burundian government had granted them.

Local integration

When conditions remain volatile and unsafe in refugees' home countries, they might stay in countries of first asylum for years—even decades. Refugees often become integrated members of their host society, contributing to the local receiving community by working in both the formal and informal economy, learning the language, and acculturating to their new home. They often reach some level of self-sufficiency and remain until their home country is safe enough to return to voluntarily.

There are three aspects of local integration: the legal process, the economic process, and the social and cultural process. These aspects play out in both formal and informal ways, and each contributes to the stability and prospering of refugees and their families.

In the early 2000s, thousands of Burundian refugees fled into Tanzania. In 2007, Tanzania announced its plan to naturalize around 220,000 Burundian refugees who had been in Tanzania since 1972. The program launched in March 2008, and 164,000 individuals applied for Tanzanian citizenship. During this local integration process, 98 percent of applications were accepted.

The government of Tanzania worked closely with UNHCR on the required relocation from settlements to sixteen regions across Tanzania to help with the absorption capacity of receiving communities. In August 2011, the Tanzanian government suspended the relocation planning and, in 2015, decided that the naturalization process would proceed without requiring relocation.

In another positive example, in 2002, Mexico gave 2,806 land titles to Guatemalan refugees in the Mexican state of Campeche. This provision of land happened in conjunction with the return of about 43,000 refugees to Guatemala.[12] The president of Mexico spoke at a ceremony, encouraging the refugees and local residents to participate in local programming to help develop this rural area of Mexico. The refugees became part of an economic improvement plan for the whole region.

Still, local integration pursued systematically by host governments is rare. In many developing nations, informal settlements and urban dwellings mark the presence of large numbers of refugees over the course of years. However, some host governments are realizing that pursuing local integration can lead to long-term solutions for persistent crises while promoting local economic development that benefits both refugees and host communities.[13] Efforts to build better relations between them, with development assistance targeting both groups, are critical.

Local integration can be a positive, durable solution, particularly in situations in which refugees have lived for more than a decade in their host countries and have no land or home to go back to. After this extended time in their host countries, refugees have often acclimated to the culture, language, and customs. In such cases, then, the legal rights afforded refugees through local integration give them the opportunity to remain where they are without fear of deportation.

Resettlement

Refugees who can neither return to their country of origin nor safely stay in their country of refuge are at times selected to be resettled to a third country. Less than 1 percent of the world's refugees are ever resettled, however, even as the resettlement need has been approximately 10 percent of the global refugee population.

In 2016, 162,500 individuals were referred for resettlement, marking a twenty-year high. Of these, 125,800 departed for their resettlement countries.[14] Thirty-seven nations engaged in these resettlement activities. However, 2017 was a difficult year as national security became a heightened concern, resulting in a decrease in resettlement slots worldwide. The UNHCR estimates that 1.2 million people are in need of resettlement in 2018, a number that remains somewhat steady compared to the previous year. Syrian refugees make up 40 percent of this population, making them the largest group in need of resettlement.[15] They are followed by refugees from the Democratic Republic of Congo (12 percent) and the Central African Republic (8 percent).[16]

The United States is considered the world's leader in refugee resettlement, having resettled the largest number of refugees over more than a decade. In 2016, for example, the United States resettled 78,340 refugees; Canada resettled 21,838; Australia, 7,502; the United Kingdom, 5,074; and Norway, 3,149.[17] In 2016, twenty-three countries naturalized refugees, with Canada reporting the highest number at 16,300 naturalizations.[18]

The United States' resettlement program was codified into law by the Refugee Act of 1980. This act stipulated that the president, in consultation with Congress, shall determine every year the number of refugees to be admitted. The act also set up a national system whereby each state has a refugee coordinator. In addition, it established a public-private partnership with various US resettlement agencies whose task is to pick up refugees at the airport and help in their initial integration, with the aid of local volunteers and community support.

While the US Refugee Resettlement Program is run by the Department of State as a foreign policy tool, the Department of Health and Human Services assists in the longer-term integration process. The resettlement program is a great example of a robust public-private partnership, as resettlement agencies bring in volunteers, in-kind donations, and private funding to match the small amount of assistance provided by the US government for initial resettlement.

Since 1980, the United States has resettled more than three million refugees representing more than forty nationalities. However, 2017 marked a departure from this historic commitment to refugee resettlement as four consecutive executive orders from the US president suspended the refugee resettlement program and banned certain nationalities from coming to the United States as immigrants. The president also set the refugee ceiling at 45,000 for fiscal year 2018, the lowest number since the Refugee Act was passed in 1980. April 1, 2018, marked the halfway point of FY18, and the United States had resettled only 10,548 refugees, even though refugee arrivals should be around 22,500 by this point to reach the 45,000-person ceiling. This means that if the United States continues on this trend, only about 20,000 refugees will be resettled in the entire fiscal year, the lowest number since 1980. As of April 1, only 44 Syrian refugees have been resettled in the US, compared to the 5,839 Syrian refugees who had been resettled in the US at the same point in FY17.

Although used sparingly, resettlement continues to offer a lifeline of protection and security for those who qualify. The US remains a needed and critical partner in this international work.

REFUGEE ASSISTANCE BEYOND RESETTLEMENT

The durable solutions discussed above are a means to provide protection by UNHCR and other countries. But a central part of global refugee policy is not only protection but also assistance in meeting the basic needs of refugees, regardless of where they are living. This assistance includes shelter, food, health care, and education. Many countries of first asylum allow refugees to access local medical care and education. In some cases, especially when refugees are confined to camps, international agencies like UNHCR, World Food Program, and others provide such assistance. International funding for such agencies is crucial so they can maintain their operations and meet refugees' basic needs. Through the Department of State's Bureau of Population, Refugees, and Migration, the United States provides direct assistance through partner organizations like UNHCR and by partnering with non-governmental organizations like World Relief, Save the Children, International Rescue Committee, World Vision, and others. Its budget is primarily split between overseas refugee assistance and the US refugee admissions program.

Increasingly, this assistance has been provided not only for refugees but for host communities as well, as they are often in need of the same basic help as are refugees. As you can imagine, tension often arises when refugees are seen as receiving more aid than the local population. Refugee assistance often falls into the gap between traditional relief and development because international agencies and host governments are both often reluctant to include refugees in traditional development programming. Currently, a shift is taking place in how traditional development actors, like USAID and the World Bank, include refugees in longer development projects. The World Bank, for example, recently provided a $2 billion financing window to help both refugee and host communities.[19] This was an effort to support low-income countries, which often host the largest number of refugees in the world.

THE CHALLENGING DYNAMICS OF REFUGEE PROTECTION

Increasing complexities in the protection of refugees are making it critical to adapt international refugee law to current crises. For example, the rise in the number of refugees in non-camp, urban settings; the millions of individuals who are stateless but not refugees and therefore lack the protection of any given country or international body; and those who are internally displaced and, thus, are not fully protected by UNHCR or other international bodies requires policies and practices that reach and protect people who face unique vulnerabilities.

As of 2016, the majority of the world's refugees lived not in refugee camps but in urban settings. While living outside camp settings can provide greater freedom of movement and self-reliance, it also presents unique challenges as refugees lack access to basic health care, education, and services and are often victims of discrimination and violence.[20] Many face the risk of arrest and detention, as well as increased vulnerability to gender-based violence and trafficking.

The UNHCR's 2009 urban refugee policy was a shift in thinking for the global community, whose protection and assistance of refugees had been based on the traditional camp setting. This new policy recognized cities as legitimate places for refugees to live, while maximizing the protection space available to urban refugees.[21] The policy emphasized the role of the state in providing primary protection while calling on local actors, like mayors and municipal authorities, to create a safe environment. The urban policy was also specific in how best to facilitate protection and assistance for refugees outside a camp setting. For example, UNHCR committed to providing reception facilities in urban areas, undertaking registration and data collection, providing refugee documentation, and carrying out Refugee Status Determinations.[22] In addition, the principle of "Age, Gender, and Diversity Mainstreaming" now informs responses to refugees, recognizing that every refugee has their own vulnerabilities, interests, needs, and capacities that need to be considered when determining what protection will look like.[23]

PROTRACTED REFUGEE SITUATIONS

When more than 25,000 refugees of the same nationality are in a given country of asylum for more than five years, it is considered a "protracted refugee situation." An estimated 11.6 million refugees, or two-thirds of refugees in 2016, are in protracted refugee situations, with most of them in developing countries.[24] Of these refugees, 4.1 million have lived in this situation for twenty years or longer.[25] It is estimated that the average duration of refugee situations has risen from nine years in 1993 to over eighteen years today. Protracted refugee situations are dynamic, however. New arrivals and returns impact the total numbers, as do situations in which one group of refugees from a specific country is smaller in number and scattered across various asylum countries but is in prolonged displacement.

Given that the majority of refugees live in some of the poorest and most unstable countries in the developing world, promoting refugee self-reliance is key. Not only does self-reliance benefit the refugees themselves, but it provides a dignified way for them to become contributing members to their host communities, strengthening the whole system. From a policy perspective, these basic elements are at play: providing refugees with physical, legal, and economic security; removing barriers to self-reliance; and creating opportunities for meaningful contribution.[26]

The legal barriers to self-reliance are some of the most difficult to overcome. Often, refugees lack the legal authority to work, which means they are unable to maintain financial self-sufficiency. Restrictions on movement mean they can't leave a camp to find work. Lack of legal access to land prevents refugees from building their own homes or growing their own food. Sustainable policy that removes these legal barriers in protracted refugee situations is critical for the long-term prospects of refugees, whether they return to their home countries or integrate into their country of first asylum. The 2009 UNHCR Executive Committee's Conclusion on Protracted Refugee Situations called upon states to act in a "spirit of international solidarity" to share the burden of refugee protection and assistance, promoting the use of all three durable solutions to improve protracted refugee situations around the world.[27]

BEYOND REFUGEES

Humanitarian crises have become more complex in the past two decades, as people flee their homes due to climate change or persecution but remain within the borders of their country. Technically, these individuals do not fall under the international protection of UNHCR or many nation-states. But UNHCR's mandate has gradually expanded to include people outside its traditional set of responsibilities and take on other groups affected by forced migration.

By definition, refugees are people who have crossed an international border, but Internally Displaced Persons (IDPs), while in many cases fleeing the same conditions as refugees, still reside in their home country. In 2016, there were more IDPs in the world than refugees, with 31.1 million people internally displaced by conflict, persecution, and disasters.[28] Because IDPs fall outside the traditional mandate of UNHCR, they can remain particularly vulnerable. The countries that are producing the majority of the world's refugees, including Syria, the Democratic Republic of Congo, and South Sudan, are also producing the greatest numbers of IDPs. An estimated 40 percent of the Syrian population, or 7.6 million people, is internally displaced.

In 2017, UNCHR laid out a comprehensive strategy to engage in solutions for IDPs. This strategy includes centralized protection, better links between refugee and IDP responses, and streamlined decision-making to IDP situations.[29] Preparing to engage early, along with changing the mindset of international entities to prevent, respond to, and resolve internal displacement, will help ensure that the needs of IDPs do not fall through the cracks.

Another group that sits outside the traditional definition of refugee is those who are stateless. A stateless person is someone who is not considered a national under the operation of any country's laws.[30] Statelessness can occur when new states are created, when there are gaps in nationality laws, or when there is discrimination against certain groups of people. Around ten million people in the world are stateless, and approximately one-third of these are children. Because they have no nationality, stateless people have difficulty accessing basic rights such as housing, employment, and education.

The Rohingya in Bangladesh, for example, are considered a stateless people because although they reside in large numbers in Myanmar, the government of Myanmar does not recognize them as Myanmarese citizens and many have been expelled in recent years. Between the end of August 2017 and early 2018, more than 647,000 Rohingya fled to Bangladesh.

Other groups of stateless individuals include the Nubians in Kenya, the Bedouin in Kuwait, and children born in the Sabah state in Borneo, Malaysia.[31]

Created in 2014, the ten-year Global Action Plan to End Statelessness focuses on four areas: identification, prevention, reduction, and protection. The plan acts to ensure that no child is born stateless by urging states to have laws that grant nationality to all children born in their territory. It removes gender discrimination in nationality laws so that women and men are treated equally regarding acquisition or retention of nationality for themselves and their children. It urges states to issue documentation of nationality. And it calls for the prevention of statelessness in the case of state succession (a successor state is a sovereign state over a territory and people that were previously under the sovereignty of another state), among other areas.[32] These steps are an effort to bring stateless populations under a plan of global protection similar to the one provided to refugees.

Assisting and protecting people forced to flee their homes requires the long-term commitment and investment of the international community. As the Secretary General of the UN, Antonio Guterres, has stated, "The protection of refugees is not only the responsibility of neighbouring States of a crisis; it is a collective responsibility of the international community."[33] While long-term solutions for refugees are ultimately political in nature, providing refugees with short-term care with an eye to durable solutions will be critical to ensuring that refugees live lives of dignity and peace in their new home environments, wherever those may be. The complex migration crises we see today are likely to continue and even increase. They will include individuals who do not fall under the traditional definition of refugee but deserve the same international protection. Our global refugee policy must be molded to fit this reality. But this is more than crisis management. It is human rights work. Refugees are the victims of political conflict and have no choice in being forced to flee for their lives, yet they often become significant contributors to the countries of asylum or resettlement that host them. Any conversation that shapes global policy decisions in the years ahead must affirm the rights, dignity, and capacity of refugees to contribute wherever they are.

Jenny Yang is the Vice President of Advocacy and Policy at World Relief. She has spent more than a decade in refugee protection, immigration policy, and human rights work, and previously worked at one of the largest political fundraising firms in Maryland. She is co-author of Welcoming the Stranger: Justice, Compassion and Truth in the Immigration Debate *(InterVarsity Press, 2009). She was named one of "50 Women to Watch" by* Christianity Today *in 2012 and "7 Leaders to Follow in 2017" by* Relevant Magazine *in 2017. Jenny is an Assistant Professor at Kilns College in Bend, Oregon, where she teaches politics, social justice, and theology. She is also on the advisory board of Christianity Today Women and on the Board of Directors for The Justice Conference.*

ENDNOTES

1   "The 1951 Refugee Convention," United Nations High Commissioner for Refugees (UNHCR), accessed April 29, 2018, http://www.unhcr. org/en-us/1951-refugee-convention.html.

2   Brian Lander and Michelle Cervantes, "UN adopts draft resolution to strengthen UNHCR's mandate for refugees," United Nations High Commissioner for Refugees (UNHCR), November 14, 2003, http://www.unhcr.org/en-us/news/latest/2003/11/3fb4e4734/ un-adopts-draft-resolution-strengthen-unhcrs-mandate-refugees.html.

3   "Convention and Protocol Relating to the Status of Refugees," United Nations High Commissioner for Refugees (UNHCR), accessed April 29, 2018, http://www.unhcr.org/en-us/3b66c2aa10.

4   "Alternatives to Camps Policy," United Nations High Commissioner for Refugees (UNHCR), accessed April 29, 2018, http://www.unhcr. org/en-us/protection/statelessness/5422b8f09/unhcr-policy-alterna- tives-camps.html.

5   "OAU Convention Governing the Specific Aspects of Refugee Prob- lems in Africa," United Nations High Commissioner for Refugees (UNHCR), accessed April 29, 2018, http://www.unhcr.org/about-us/ background/45dc1a682/oau-convention-governing-specific-aspects-ref- ugee-problems-africa-adopted.html.

6   "OUA Convention."

7   "OUA Convention."

8   "Global Trends: Forced Displacement in 2016," UNHCR, accessed April 29, 2018, http://www.unhcr.org/globaltrends2016/.

9   "RAHA: Refugee Affected and Hosting Areas Programme," UNHCR Islamabad, accessed April 29, 2018, http://unhcrpk.org/wp-content/ uploads/2013/12/RAHA-Brochure-June-20161.pdf.

10   "RAHA."

11   "Impact Evaluation of PRM humanitarian assistance to the repa- triation and reintegration of Burundi refugees (2003-2008)," United States Department of State, accessed April 29, 2018, https://relief- web.int/report/burundi/impact-evaluation-prm-humanitarian-assis- tance-repatriation-and-reintegration-burundi.

12   "Mexico: Local Integration in Campeche," UNHCR, May 10, 2002, http://www.unhcr.org/en-us/news/briefing/2002/5/3cdbadd311/mexi-co-local-integration-campeche.html.

13   Karen Jacobsen, "Local Integration: The Forgotten Solution," *Migration Information Source*, October 1, 2003, https://www.migrationpoli-cy.org/article/local-integration-forgotten-solution.

14   "Global Resettlement Needs," UNHCR, accessed April 29, 2018, http://www.unhcr.org/en-us/protection/resettlement/593a88f27/un-hcr-projected-global-resettlement-needs-2018.html.

15   "Global."

16   "Global."

17   "Global."

18   "Global Trends," 28.

19   "Eight Countries Eligible for New IDA Financing to Support Refugees and Hosts," World Bank acessed April 29, 2018, http://www.world-bank.org/en/topic/fragilityconflictviolence/brief/eight-countries-eligi-ble-for-new-ida-financing-to-support-refugees-and-hosts.

20   For more information, see UNHCR's 2014 policy on alternative to camps. http://www.unhcr.org/en-us/protection/stateless-ness/5422b8f09/unhcr-policy-alternatives-camps.html.

21   "UNHCR policy on refugee protection and solutions in urban ar-eas," UNHCR, accessed April 29, 2018, http://www.refworld.org/do-cid/4ab8e7f72.html.

22   "UNHCR policy."

23   "UNHCR Age, Gender, and Diversity Policy: Working with people and communities for equality and protection," UNHCR, June 1, 2011, http://www.unhcr.org/en-us/protection/women/4e7757449/unhcr-age-gender-diversity-policy-working-people-communities-equali-ty-protection.html.

24   "Global Trends," 22.

25   "Global Trends," 22.

26   Executive Committee of the High Commissioner's Programme, 30th Meeting: Protracted Refugee Situations," UNHCR, accessed April 29, 2018, http://www.unhcr.org/en-us/excom/standcom/40c982172/pro-tracted-refugee-situations.html.

27   "Conclusion on Protracted Refugee Situations ," UNHCR, accessed April 29, 2018, http://www.unhcr.org/en-us/excom/exconc/4b332b-ca9/conclusion-protracted-refugee-situations.html.

28   "On the GRID: Internal Displacement in 2016," Internal Displacement Monitoring Center, accessed April 29, 2018, http://www.internal-dis-placement.org/global-report/grid2017/.

29   "Operational Review of UNHCR's Engagement in Situations of Inter-nal Displacement," UNHCR, September 2017, http://www.unhcr.org/en-us/protection/idps/5a02d6887/operational-review-unhcrs-engage-ment-situations-internal-displacement.html.

30   "Ending Statelessness," UNHCR, accessed April 29, 2018, http://www.unhcr.org/en-us/stateless-people.html.

31   "Factbox: Stateless Groups around the World," *Reuters*, August 23, 2011, https://www.reuters.com/article/us-stateless-groups/factbox-stateless-groups-around-the-world-idUSTRE77M2AS20110823.

32   "Global Action Plan to End Statelessness," UNHCR, November 4, 2014, http://www.refworld.org/docid/545b47d64.html.

33   "Global Trends."

4

A NETWORK OF CARE

THE CRITICAL ROLE OF RESETTLEMENT AGENCIES

BY SARAH KRAUSE, MS

*If the whole body were an eye, where would the hearing be? If the whole
body were hearing, where would the sense of smell be? But as it is, God
arranged the members in the body, each one of them, as he chose. If all
were a single member, where would the body be? As it is, there are many
members, yet one body. (1 Corinthians 12:17-20)*

I discovered my part in the body of refugee work as an intern with Human
Rights First, then known as the Lawyers' Committee for Human Rights, in
Washington, DC. The internship had been arranged for me by the American
Studies Program, a program of the Council for Christian Colleges and
Universities that seeks to connect students to institutions impacting issues
in public policy and strategic communication. As part of my internship, I
was asked to conduct research for an asylum case. I was sorting through
paperwork and organizing some documents when I stumbled across a file on
Sierra Leone. What I found in that file changed me.

I saw pictures of women and children with stumps for limbs. Under one
picture was a caption: "I had to bury my own hand." As that sank in, I
came across another picture in the file, this one of a four-year-old boy, with
a caption that read, "A family's only survivor." The picture was part of an
article that told of how the boy had been at home with sixteen members of
his family when rebels attacked, accusing them of backing the government.
This little boy was shot in the arm. Everyone else in his family was killed.

Sometime later, a nurse came to clear the home of dead bodies. She heard whimpering coming from under one of the bodies and moved it to find this little boy lying in a fetal position. As the only survivor, the boy had to identify the bodies of his family, including his father. The article noted that he was so traumatized by the incident that he didn't speak or eat for weeks.

It was the image of this little boy in his soccer T-shirt and sweatpants that first made war real to me. I remember thinking, "I have to do something." My twenty-one-year-old self wanted to fly to Sierra Leone to save him, to bring him home with me and care for him myself. But just a few weeks later, I was led in another direction, one that has given me the opportunity to care for countless little boys—and mothers and fathers and families. I attended an ecumenical conference and was seated next to an elderly Presbyterian couple. I told them about this little boy and my conviction to do something to help people like him. They told me about their church's experience with refugee resettlement. And just like that, I knew what I wanted to do with my life.

Fewer than 1 percent of the world's refugee population will have the opportunity to resettle in a third country (their home country counting as the first; the country to which they fled counting as the second) like the United States. This is due to the small number of countries that take part in the United Nations High Commissioner for Refugees (UNHCR) resettlement program, as well as the very limited number of resettlement slots made available by these countries. Of those participating in UNHCR's resettlement program, the United States, Canada, Australia, and certain Nordic countries accept the largest number of refugees, and while this should be a great source of pride for these countries, it is important to note that the numbers they accept are only a fraction of those being hosted by (in contrast to being resettled in) countries such as Turkey (2.9 million), Pakistan (1.4 million), and Lebanon (1.1 million).[1] The international effort to coordinate the movement of millions and millions of people—often without the benefit of clear communication or transportation resources—is nothing short of astonishing.

By now, you've read enough to know that refugees are those who have been forced from their home country due to a fear of persecution based on their race, religion, national origin, political opinion, or membership in a particular social group. You know that refugee status is typically conferred by the UNHCR, the largest refugee-serving agency in the world. And you know that this process can be a long one, due in part to UNHCR's limited resources. Now present in 130 countries,[2] the UNHCR works in partnership with several hundred non-government organizations around the world to provide protection and relief to refugees well before they are able to be resettled. These organizations—both those that work with refugees in-country and those that work in the countries that accept them for resettlement—serve as the backbone of the world's response to the refugee crisis.

CREATING A NETWORK

Before the US Refugee Admissions Program existed, there were resettlement agencies. Although not called that at the time, they sprang up throughout the United States in response to Europe's refugee crisis in the late 1800s. One of the first of these agencies was the Hebrew Immigrant Aid Society (HIAS). Founded in 1881, HIAS partnered with American Jews to provide welcome and aid to Jews fleeing pogroms in Russia and Eastern Europe. Church World Service (CWS), another faith-based resettlement agency, began as a response to what was occurring in war-torn Europe. Seventeen denominations joined "to do in partnership what none of us could hope to do as well alone."[3] For instance, CWS collected crops from farmers across the United States and brought them to ports on the East Coast by train. These same trains then carried refugees arriving by ship in New York to towns across the US, linking them with churches that would provide them assistance in getting settled. By 1946, CWS, HIAS, and other resettlement agencies had assisted thousands of refugees resettling to the United States.

This number increased significantly after the fall of Vietnam in 1975. Over the course of a few months, more than 130,000 Vietnamese "boat people" were resettled to the United States; eventually, more than 800,000 Vietnamese people came after surviving not only the war but harrowing travel across the ocean as well. For many churches in the US, this was their first direct experience with refugee resettlement. This was also when Congress determined that the country should have a more structured response to forced migration, so it established the Refugee Act of 1980. Through this act, the Federal Refugee Resettlement Program was created to provide for the effective resettlement of refugees and to assist them in achieving economic self-sufficiency as quickly as possible after arrival in the

United States. To accomplish this, the US government engaged with many of the agencies that had already been providing service to refugees.

Today, the Department of State's Bureau of Population, Refugees, and Migration contracts with just nine nonprofit resettlement agencies, six of them faith-based and all of them selected through an annual competitive process, to provide these services. These nine agencies are Church World Service, Episcopal Migration Ministries, Ethiopian Community Development Council, Hebrew Immigrant Aid Society, International Rescue Committee, Lutheran Immigration and Refugee Service, US Committee for Refugees and Immigrants, US Conference of Catholic Bishops, and World Relief. Each one has affiliate offices around the country. These agencies must re-apply with the State Department every year to demonstrate that they continue to be private, nonprofit organizations with the capacity to resettle refugees.

Resettlement agencies play a critical role in the placement of refugees in communities throughout the United States. At meetings convened by the Department of State and the Refugee Processing Center, representatives of the resettlement agencies review basic biographic information of refugees approved for resettlement and determine with which agency each refugee should be resettled. The placement decisions are made in consultation with agency affiliates and take into consideration factors like the location of any family members or friends, language capacity, availability of medical support (if needed), and the capacity of the local affiliate.

The locations of these affiliates are also intentional and carefully determined. Affiliates of the nine resettlement agencies are located in more than 150 communities[4] throughout the United States—some in large metropolitan areas, others in more rural communities or small cities. The communities are proposed by the resettlement agencies and approved by the Department of State. A variety of factors go into choosing a community, including economic opportunities, housing availability, existing ethnic communities, and the possibility of community support such as welcoming faith communities. It's important to note that there is no such thing as a "perfect" resettlement community; each community has its advantages and disadvantages.

Over time, the affiliate network expands and contracts based on the number of refugees arriving to the US, the countries from which they are coming, and the ability and willingness of the community itself to receive arrivals.[5] An affiliate may or may not have the same name as its headquarter agency—some are part of the overall structure of the resettlement agency, while others are independent organizations that subcontract with the resettlement agency through a memorandum of agreement or understanding. While the way in which affiliates relate to their headquarters differs, all are held to the same standards laid out through the Reception and Placement Program Cooperative Agreement and are monitored by both the resettlement agency headquarters and the Department of State to ensure compliance and consistency of care.

Once a placement decision is made for a refugee, information about the affiliate, also known as the "sponsoring agency," is relayed to a Resettlement Support Center overseas that assists in the refugee's processing. These organizations work with the International Organization for Migration to ensure that the refugee travels to the United States with all required documentation. All of this is done in close collaboration with the Bureau of Population, Refugees, and Migration of the Department of State and the Citizenship and Immigration Services agency of the Department of Homeland Security.

The initial resettlement services are detailed in the Cooperative Agreement, along with the timeframe for providing them. These services really kick in as soon as a refugee arrives in the United States. Refugees are greeted at the airport by a representative of the resettlement agency and/or a family member or friend. This is a powerful experience. The refugee journey to the US is a long and arduous one that, in many cases, began decades before. As a result, the airport greeting is an emotional experience, creating strong bonds between the arriving refugees and those welcoming them. Joseph, the first refugee I ever greeted at the airport, said to me months later, "You, Sarah, are a part of our family. You were with us from the beginning. You picked us up from the airport. I cannot forget your face."

From the airport, the refugee is transported to his or her apartment furnished with all items mandated through the Reception and Placement Cooperative Agreement. (The Department of State is very specific about the items that must be provided—even mandating the number of trash cans that have to be in the home!) The refugee receives an initial home and personal safety orientation and is then left to rest. Shortly after, the real work begins. Newly arrived refugees quickly obtain a Social Security card and apply for available benefits. Children are enrolled in school, and adults are enrolled in English Language Learner (ELL) classes and employment services.

The Reception and Placement program, funded by the Department of State, is focused on initial resettlement and, as a result, is limited to the first three months after arrival. Depending on the community, the refugee might be provided with other, ongoing services including language classes, employment guidance, and social services, often with funds through the Department of Health and Human Services' Office of Refugee Resettlement.

A PUBLIC-PRIVATE PARTNERSHIP

All of this good work calls for financial and human resources. On the financial side, affiliates receive a very limited amount of money from the Department of State, the majority of which must be spent directly on the refugee's behalf. These funds are used to provide essential resettlement needs like housing, furniture, groceries, and seasonally appropriate clothing. The remaining amount can be used to pay for the affiliate's operational expenses, including casework staff and office space. These funds are rarely sufficient to cover the full work of an organization. The Department of State is aware that the funding is inadequate, but with the help of other nonprofit organizations and volunteers, as well as the fundraising efforts of affiliates, resettlement agencies are equipped to continue to provide the services crucial to a smooth transition for refugees.

One of the pervasive public concerns over refugee resettlement is the cost to taxpayers. As with so much of the conversation around refugees, there is a great deal of misinformation about the financial support the government provides to resettled refugees. Many people are shocked to learn that the cost of a refugee's travel to the United States comes in the form of a forty-six-month, no-interest loan which the refugee is expected to repay. The loan payments are collected by the headquarters of the receiving resettlement agency over time, with the first bill sent approximately six months after the refugee's arrival. While well-intentioned churches may be tempted to repay the loan for the refugees, resettlement agencies discourage this, as the process teaches refugees about the US loan system and supports them in establishing good credit. While the vast majority of loans are repaid in full, those that are not repaid are turned over for collection to the International

Organization for Migration. Money received through loan collection supports refugee resettlement. Below is a letter received by the resettlement agency Church World Service from one of the refugees they resettled in 2012. Identifying information has been redacted.

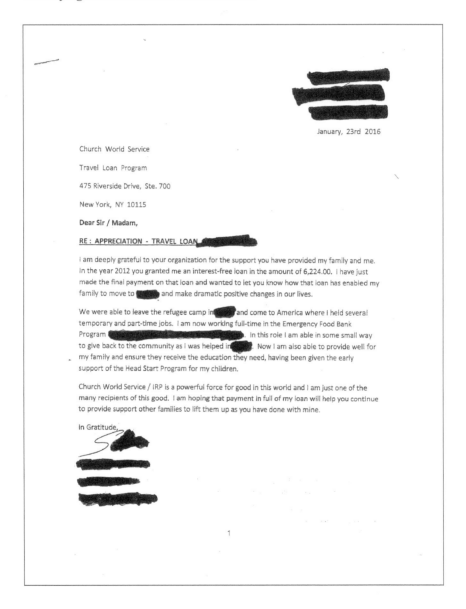

January, 23rd 2016

Church World Service

Travel Loan Program

475 Riverside Drive, Ste. 700

New York, NY 10115

Dear Sir / Madam,

RE : APPRECIATION - TRAVEL LOAN

I am deeply grateful to your organization for the support you have provided my family and me. In the year 2012 you granted me an interest-free loan in the amount of 6,224.00. I have just made the final payment on that loan and wanted to let you know how that loan has enabled my family to move to ▒▒▒ and make dramatic positive changes in our lives.

We were able to leave the refugee camp in ▒▒▒ and come to America where I held several temporary and part-time jobs. I am now working full-time in the Emergency Food Bank Program ▒▒▒▒▒▒▒▒▒▒▒. In this role I am able in some small way to give back to the community as I was helped in ▒▒▒. Now I am also able to provide well for my family and ensure they receive the education they need, having been given the early support of the Head Start Program for my children.

Church World Service / IRP is a powerful force for good in this world and I am just one of the many recipients of this good. I am hoping that payment in full of my loan will help you continue to provide support other families to lift them up as you have done with mine.

In Gratitude,

1

Beginning with the cultural orientation refugees go through before they leave for the United States—and continuing for the first few months after their arrival—the focus of resettlement is always on helping the refugee become self-sufficient. The majority of refugees are able to find jobs and make enough money to move off of public assistance within six months after their arrival. Considering all that refugees endure prior to their resettlement, that's no small accomplishment.

THE CRUCIAL WORK OF CO-SPONSORS

As mentioned earlier, the Reception and Placement Program is a public-private partnership, with the government providing a limited amount of funding and resettlement agencies contributing significant cash and/or in-kind resources to supplement this funding. Resettlement agencies accomplish this in a number of ways, including the use of co-sponsorships. A local co-sponsor is defined by the Cooperative Agreement as "an established community group which has accepted in a written agreement with an Agency responsibility to provide, or ensure the provision of, reception and placement services to certain refugees sponsored by an Agency. Individuals or informal groups may not serve as local co-sponsors. Local co-sponsors differ from volunteers in that they agree in writing to accept responsibility for performing certain services required in this agreement."[6] More simply, co-sponsor groups serve as friends, guides, and advocates to arriving refugee families. While co-sponsors have a written agreement to provide services, it's important to note that the agreement is a moral one, not a legal one. Ultimately, the responsibility for service provision lies with the resettlement agency.

At the same time, co-sponsors are crucial partners in this work. My first full-time job following my college internship with Human Rights First was Sponsorship Developer with the Church of the Brethren General Board, an affiliate of Church World Service. As Sponsorship Developer, I was responsible for encouraging churches and other faith communities in the Maryland area to consider co-sponsorship of arriving refugee families. I was able to witness firsthand the impact co-sponsorship has on arriving refugee families. One family we worked with included a fourteen-year-old girl who arrived pregnant. She'd been taken advantage of by an adult male in the refugee camp prior to her departure. Through the support of the church, she was able to continue her high school education. Her connection to her sponsoring community was so strong that she named her daughter after the chair of the church's co-sponsorship committee.

The church, too, was changed by this experience. Co-sponsorship connects churches with new ethnic communities in their area, allows them to better understand the challenges in navigating social service systems, and reinvigorates church members through hands-on volunteer opportunities.

Even churches and community organizations in areas that don't offer direct services to refugees can partner with affiliates to join in this work. Rutgers Presbyterian is an affluent church on the Upper West Side of Manhattan. In 2015, Andrew Stehlik, the church's Senior Pastor, challenged those sitting in the pews to join efforts to aid refugees. That fall, several church members and friends began meeting as the Refugee Task Force and donated money to refugee-serving organizations like Church World Service. The task force also learned that Church World Service offered opportunities for churches to become co-sponsors, and they quickly agreed that they wanted to be of service and have a direct connection with a family.

The only challenge was that, while Rutgers Presbyterian is located in New York City, CWS doesn't resettle refugees there, due in part to the high cost of living. That meant the church would be connected with a family outside their immediate area. Still, the group agreed that any challenges would be worth working through. They felt they had a responsibility to respond and agreed to co-sponsor a Syrian family being resettled in nearby New Jersey. Within six months of co-sponsoring their first family, the church volunteered to co-sponsor a second family, who arrived in February 2017.

Dave Mammen, Director of Administration, Programs, and Special Projects at Rutgers Presbyterian, describes the church's experience in this way:

> It has been a wonderful and very meaningful experience for our church and all those involved. Our co-sponsorship has created many opportunities for volunteers to be of service by preparing apartments for the families' arrival; helping family members enroll in benefit programs and school; teaching English and tutoring in other subjects; helping family members find jobs; etc. Many others have donated goods and money to help the families.
>
> Our partnership with both families will continue until they achieve self-sufficiency, and our efforts to assist new immigrants have broadened. Church members who are attorneys have volunteered at legal clinics to help DACA Dreamers, [asylum seekers,] and others. Others serve on a

committee convened by a local synagogue to help refugees, asylees, and those on Special Immigrant Visas to find jobs. Church staff and friends have collected and delivered donated household items to refugees and asylees referred by several resettlement agencies. We have also taken every opportunity offered to share our experience with others, speaking at many churches and synagogues around New York.

These efforts have helped us establish new relations with many other churches and synagogues, as well as neighbors and friends of good will. Of course, we understand that our efforts are almost insignificant in light of the vast worldwide refugee crisis. Yet we feel blessed to have the resources and opportunity to help. We hope to co-sponsor another family soon.[7]

There are countless models for how churches and other organizations can partner with resettlement agencies. Volunteers can assist with English language training, job searches, homework help, or community orientation. Even if direct interaction with refugees isn't possible, communities can offer cash or in-kind contributions like household goods. It's best for these donations to go to the resettlement agency, rather than directly to a family, so that the resettlement agency can demonstrate to the US government that there is support in the local community—this is one of the factors the government considers when it reviews its partnerships every year. It also helps to ensure that the assistance is given to the refugee family in greatest need.

Finally, individuals can advocate for just immigration policies. Each resettlement agency maintains an advocacy arm, funded privately for this purpose. While some advocacy staff are based in Washington, DC, others travel throughout the country to better understand local issues and to support the advancement of just policy at local and state levels.

No matter what kind of help churches offer, the benefits to both the refugees and the partnering community are invaluable. When volunteers connect with refugees in their communities, they gain a greater understanding of international affairs, the US Refugee Admissions Program, and local poverty. This information makes church members more effective advocates, not only for the refugees with whom they work but for all displaced people.[8]

EXPANDING THE NETWORK

In addition to national refugee-serving agencies and their local affiliates, numerous public organizations provide support to refugees. These include public schools that provide education to refugee children, GED providers, and job training centers. Depending on the location and the number of refugees resettled to a particular area, these agencies may receive government funding specific to refugees. It is also possible that they won't. If you're interested in providing support to these institutions and those whom they serve, seek them out and find out how you can be of help.

Throughout the country there are also local Ethnic Community-Based Organizations (ECBOs), formerly known as Mutual Assistance Associations. ECBOs are nonprofit organizations whose governing boards are composed primarily of refugees or former refugees; such organizations provide social services to support refugees in integrating into their new communities. The services provided vary depending on the needs of the community but include such things as interpretation and translation, case management, emergency assistance, and youth mentoring.

Finally, thousands of grassroots groups across the country provide direct service to refugees. Some of these are registered 501(c)3 nonprofit organizations while others are informal coalitions of faith communities. These groups can play a critical role in ensuring that gaps in services are filled and that newcomers are supported.

CREATING A WARM WELCOME

While direct services are critical to a refugee's success, so, too, is the general welcome they receive from the community. This is especially true today. In the cultural orientation refugees receive prior to their arrival to the United States, many now share that their greatest fear regarding resettlement is that they won't be welcomed by their host communities or that they will be "sent back" to the country from which they fled.

Communities can access tools and training to cultivate greater acceptance of refugees. Welcoming America, an agency launched in 2009, provides a roadmap to assist communities across the country in being more inclusive. Their website, welcomingamerica.org, includes toolkits and other resources for helping communities. Institutions, including local governments, can be certified by the agency as "welcoming" and gain access to a network of other institutions across the country also seeking to become more welcoming; can participate in learning exchanges; and can be recognized for their efforts to become inclusive.

Refugees Are Welcome is another large collective of faith-based and civic organizations that has banded together to create additional resources for communities. Their website, refugeesarewelcome.org, is a clearinghouse for tools, including signs, charts, advocacy information sheets, and webinars on how to grow effective partnerships.

The question of how to create a better welcome for arriving refugees is not unique to the United States. It is being faced by countries throughout Europe as well. In Bulgaria, researcher and policy analyst Zvezda Vankova established the Multi Kulti Collective (MKC). Based in the capital of Sofia, MKC works on issues of community development, civic participation, solidarity, and integration of migrants and refugees. One of the more well-known aspects of MKC's work is the Multi Kulti Map, which illustrates the diversity of Bulgaria's culture and cuisine. Using the map, individuals can find authentic ethnic restaurants and food stores owned by Bulgarians, refugees, and immigrants from more than twenty countries. The stories of these owners, including why they came to Bulgaria and what they miss most about their home countries, have been collected and illustrated by artists in an effort to build community. The Multi Kulti Map has been recognized as a best practice by the European Union, and in 2015, it grew to include six additional Bulgarian cities.

There are many agencies working through a variety of means to ensure that the world's refugee crisis is addressed. As we respond to Christ's call to care for the poor, the widowed, the orphaned, and the stranger at the gate, let us be mindful of what services currently exist and prayerfully consider how we might support these efforts or what we might do to fill the gap. Let us work together as one body.

Sarah Krause, MS, has more than 18 years of national and international experience with refugees and immigrants. She has served as a Sponsorship Developer, Caseworker, Program Coordinator and Director of a local affiliate and later worked in the Church World Service-administered Resettlement Support Centers in both Accra, Ghana, and Nairobi, Kenya, overseeing the processing of refugee applications for resettlement to the United States and the cultural orientation refugees received prior to travel. She served as Senior Director of Programs with Church World Service, administering the agency's programming in the United States, Africa, and the Caribbean, and has worked with the International Rescue Committee providing training to European countries on best practices in refugee integration, and the International Organization for Migration in the development of a cultural orientation curriculum for refugees resettling to Romania. She lives in New York City where she works as an independent consultant specializing in fundraising and refugee and immigrant affairs.

ENDNOTES

1   United Nations High Commissioner for Refugees, "Figures at a Glance, UNHCR, April 2018, http://www.unhcr.org/en-us/figures-at-a-glance.html.

2   UNHCR, "Where We Work," UNHCR, April 2018, http://www.unhcr.org/en-us/where-we-work.html.

3   "We Are All America," Church World Service, April 2018, https://www.weareallusa.org/church_world_service.

4   "FY2016 Reception and Placement Program Affiliate Sites," Refugee Processing Center, April 2018, https://static1.squarespace.com/static/580e4274e58c624696efadc6/t/583c76e7440243877af-f59ef/1480357955543/.

5   A recent listing of affiliates in the United States can be found at http://www.wrapsnet.org/rp-agency-contacts/.

6   "FY2010 Reception and Placement Basic Terms of the Cooperative Agreement Between the Government of the United States of America and the (Name of Organization)," United States Department of State, April 2018, https://2009-2017.state.gov/j/prm/releases/sample/181175.htm.

7   Dave Mammen, written statement to author, January 21, 2018.

8   To learn more about the nine resettlement agencies and other national refugee-serving agencies, such as the Multi-faith Alliance for Syrian Refugees, visit Refugee Council USA (RCUSA) at www.rcusa.org. RCUSA is a coalition of twenty-five US-based non-governmental organizations dedicated to refugee protection, welcome, and excellence in the US refugee resettlement program.

5

FACING OUR HISTORY

OTHERNESS, RACE, AND THE AMERICAN CHALLENGE

BY HALIMA Z. ADAMS*

INDIANAPOLIS, INDIANA

On a sunny April day, I found myself in southwest Indianapolis with a colleague as part of our work as monitors for a national refugee resettlement agency. We conduct site visits to all of our local partner organizations, checking on the quality of support and services provided, which are mostly funded by federal government programs, and seeing how newcomers are faring. We were at an apartment complex to visit a Congolese family of nine who had arrived in the United States eight months earlier, finally resettled after years of displacement and uncertainty.

We were glad to find that the family felt safe. They were grateful for the opportunity to create a home and a new life in Indianapolis, but the father was worried about their monthly expenses and his children's transition to their new schools. He and his wife were still trying to figure out childcare options for their preschooler and wondering how they would balance working full time and learning English while managing their busy household. We encouraged the family to persevere, reminding them of the courage and fortitude they had demonstrated during their protracted

*Disclaimer: *The information and views expressed within this essay are solely the experiences, thoughts, and research of the author and referenced authors, publications, and data sources. They do not represent Church World Service, US government bodies, or any other institution acting in a formal capacity.*

displacement in East Africa. They had already survived so much. As we prepared to go, we assured them that our local partner would continue working with them to make sure they were cared for and felt welcomed in their new community.

My coworker and I left the apartment and walked toward the parking lot. We exchanged smiles and *salaam*s with a group of Middle Eastern women sitting in the courtyard grass, chatting and enjoying the sunshine of the burgeoning Midwestern spring. Glancing across the courtyard, I noticed a Confederate flag draped over the balcony railing of one of the apartments. The flag, a dark symbol of racial oppression and rebellion against the US government, waved in the breeze, casually reminding the women gathered below that they might not be granted a welcome everywhere.

Indianapolis serves as an interesting example of the tensions inherent in any discussion about refugees. Established as a Union stronghold and strategic base during the Civil War, Indianapolis served as a supply station and training camp for northern troops. Locals volunteered to serve as Union soldiers; Indianapolis doctors and nurses provided medical treatment to soldiers; and citizens provided clothing, food, and shelter to traveling Union families and troops. Indianapolis managed one of four prisons for captured Confederate soldiers during and after the Civil War, and local citizens and Union supporters helped with that too. Despite their opposition to the Confederacy, they mobilized resources and services to supply Southern prisoners with humanitarian assistance such as clothing, food, medical care, and supplies to survive cold northern winters. Indianapolis citizens actively rejected the Confederacy and what it represented. But now, more than 150 years later, at least one individual in the city still proudly supported the other side.

Despite the Union victory over a century ago, representations of the Confederacy's ideas remain a part of modern political ideology and expressions of freedom, heritage, and identity. The use of the Confederate flag by white-supremacist and white-power organizations is grounded in its connection to the belief that white people are superior to black and other non-white people in terms of class, race, and status. In his essay "The First White President," author Ta-Nehisi Coates highlights the necessity of this premise: "On the eve of secession, Jefferson Davis, the eventual president of the Confederacy, pushed the [concept of a white democratic union] further, arguing that such equality between the white working class and further, arguing that such equality between the white working class and white oligarchs could not exist at all without black slavery."[1] Simply put, Confederate heritage and identity could only be built and sustained through the active and continuous dehumanization and oppression of African Americans and other non-white populations.

Standing in that apartment parking lot in a predominantly white, working-class neighborhood in southern Indianapolis, I wondered whether these women even knew about the Confederacy, let alone its unique brand of patriotism. I'm certain their immediate concerns mirrored those of their fellow Congolese neighbors—improving their English language skills, learning to drive on US highways, surviving their first Midwestern winter, and working tirelessly to ensure that their children received a sound education and had opportunities to succeed. Whether or not they knew what the Confederate flag stood for, as a refugee protection advocate and a black American, I certainly did.

The flag was originally created during a war fought to reject people like me, to delegitimize my existence and full rights as a human being in the United States. And here it was, its energy reframed and redirected at a fresh group—refugees.

For those of us who work in the field of refugee protection and resettlement, the growing public anti-refugee sentiment of the last two decades—and the amplification of that sentiment in the last two years—is a stunning turn away from what has historically been a fairly uncontroversial system of diplomacy and support for displaced people. Yet, in so many ways this response is not unexpected when we look at America's fraught history of racism. The fear and concern that is stirred when the topic of refugee resettlement comes up is actually a very familiar narrative.

THE POWER OF FEAR

Foreign-born residents make up a fraction of the US population—about 42 million out of some 323 million, total. Despite their relatively small numbers, people who come here from other countries are depicted as equal parts victim and champion, perpetrator and vanquisher of American culture and society, depending on who creates the narrative. To hear from some sources, refugees are the cause of all the United States' societal ills: high unemployment rates, low wages for the working class, a strain on public assistance programs, a siphon on resources for "real" Americans. To some, newcomers represent moral erosion, spread drugs and violence, are a threat to the nation's inherent Christian values, and are religious extremists who bring the threat of terrorism. In short, from this perspective foreigners are a moral, physical, and cultural threat to the United States and its citizenry. Assuming it's all true, 13 percent of the US population wields the power to create widespread chaos and malaise. *Mabrouk*.[2]

To safeguard the country, the current presidential administration has proposed building a wall along the 1,954-mile US/Mexico border. It has implemented restrictive refugee and asylum policies that have drastically reduced an individual's right to protection and family reunification. In 2017, it effectively halted refugee admissions, reversing a 42-year-old bipartisan federal process of developing merit- or needs-based immigration policies, and implemented additional security measures for the already–most heavily vetted individuals entering the country.

The primary messaging around refugees seems to be propped up by two poles: 1) newcomers are taking our jobs, and 2) newcomers don't have jobs and are living off of taxpayers. Yet, somewhere in between we find the lived experience of actual newcomers. Most of the refugees resettled through national agencies like Church World Service and World Relief find jobs at local warehouses, restaurant kitchens, fast-food chains, meat processing factories, landscaping companies, or in custodial positions at hotels or hospitals. The work is physically demanding and the hours long and varied, with pay hovering around or slightly above minimum wage. Due to their limited English language skills, their immediate need to maintain households, their lack of US work experience, and/or a lack of access to other professional options, newcomers begin at the bottom of the workforce, regardless of the work they did in their home country. Your cab driver might have been a restaurant owner in Syria; the person cleaning your hotel room could have been a surgeon at home in Cuba; the cashier at the small market down the street might have been an interpreter for US military personnel in Afghanistan.

In some communities, these newcomers are seen as workforce competition, stealing valuable jobs from other low-income job-seekers. But for the newcomers themselves, employment is a way to support their families both in the United States and back home, a means to save money to purchase a minivan or a house, and a stepping stone toward one day moving back into their previous profession. Like any American, newcomers see work as a way to maintain their dignity and ability to make their own decisions. Work is a means to achieve their economic goals and become contributing members of a community.

Returning home from work, newcomers live among other low-income residents in apartments or rental homes often close to public bus routes, jobs, shopping centers, public schools, and fellow members of their ethnic community. Resettlement requirements also ensure that newcomers are housed where they can begin paying their rent within three months of arrival. Due to a combination of their initial lack of resources, including US credit and an employment history, as well as property owners' reluctance to rent to newcomers, those who have recently arrived in the US are relegated to developing small communities over time. These communities provide people with familiarity and in-kind support, such as exchanging food, information, and childcare; arranging work carpools; and strengthening cultural bonds. At the same time, these communities can become insular, leaving newcomers with limited access to external local resources, networks, and opportunities to choose what kind of neighborhood is best for them.

As a result, the public perception of refugees is often that they aren't interested in integrating into their new communities. They remain strangers—others—in the places they've been resettled. This becomes a kind of vicious circle of assumptions. Many Americans have never met someone from Afghanistan, Bhutan, El Salvador, Somalia, or Sudan. When refugees from those places move into town but seem to keep to themselves and their own community, it reinforces the notion that they aren't really members of the broader community, that they aren't interested in being Americans. This tends to breed fear and distrust, which is too often affirmed by the notions of Islamophobia and racism prevalent in the media and political discourse. This gets distilled down to a simple equation: newcomers are undereducated and poor, from Muslim countries with religious extremist ideology, whose culture and values are far from American. These perceptions can leave newcomers even more isolated and can solidify the perceived division between them and the people long settled in their new communities.

Yet, over and over again we see the resilience of refugees who have survived much worse than the unfounded fears of their neighbors. As newcomers religious beliefs, and displacement experiences with their new neighbors. Although five years of residency are required before newcomers can apply for citizenship, many enter civic life soon after arrival. Some become community leaders and speakers, visiting churches, civic organizations, or their local congressional representatives in state capitols or Washington, DC. Some lobby government leaders to protect US policies that welcome immigrants and refugees. Still others are elected to local government positions. Overseas, refugees often spend decades shaping their "refugee" identity through the formal resettlement process and in everyday life in camps, villages, or urban environments. Once resettled in the US, that label and role morphs from active victim of displacement to agent of change. It can be a powerful paradigm shift: as refugees craft and share their narratives and testimonials, they can affect political change and educate their local communities about themselves and their experience of the world. But that remains an uphill climb.

CREATING THE OTHER

The bias against refugees and other immigrants didn't begin with the 2016 presidential campaign. By way of a recent example, at the height of the Syrian civil war in 2015, Indiana's then-governor, Mike Pence, issued a directive preventing state agencies from distributing federal assistance funds to refugee resettlement agencies working with Syrians. Pence cited national security concerns as a reason for withholding resettlement services to Syrian newcomers in Indiana. One Indiana refugee resettlement agency, Exodus Refugee Immigration, sued the State of Indiana for violation of the Civil Rights Act. Exodus and the Indiana ACLU (American Civil Liberties Union) claimed that the directive discriminated against Syrians based on their nationality, a violation of equal protection laws. Three years later, a US district judge agreed with the ACLU and Exodus, issuing a permanent injunction against the State of Indiana and the head of the state funding agency, the Indiana Family and Social Services Administration.[3] Although the State of Indiana was not victorious, Kansas, Texas, Maine, and New Jersey have all followed suit and withdrawn from administering federal refugee resettlement services since 2015.

The fear of the foreigner seems to be heightened in this time of nonstop news coverage and political rhetoric. But the need to vilify the "other" is age-old. For just a moment, let's step into the study of personal identity.

age-old. For just a moment, let's step into the study of personal identity. Introduced by eighteenth-century German thinker George Wilhelm Friedrich Hegel, the notion of the "other" stems from our concept of the self. Recognizing otherness results from identifying and classifying things in a relational manner. A person's individual sense of awareness is based on, or viewed through, the differences or alternatives we see in other individuals and the world.[4] In other words, I know I am me and not you when I notice the ways in which we are different from each other. From a sociological perspective, *otherness* becomes the way we construct social groups and communities. We are "us" and they are "them." Societies cultivate identities in relation to other societies. Identity, then, shapes and is shaped by an established social order—it is relational and can only be defined and affirmed by the presence of the other. But within this relationship, there is an inherent power struggle. For one group to have any sense of cohesion and unity, it has to hold itself over and above other groups, at least in some way.

Now here's where it gets messy. Professor Edward Said, who developed the academic field of post-colonial studies, wrote about the ways Europe and the West have used this idea of otherness to justify colonialism and its imperial pursuits. In the colonializing mentality, the East, or the "Orient," for example, was considered a monolithic entity, and Eastern culture, history, religion, and communities were seen as less valuable than those of the West.[5] This same thinking is apparent in Christopher Columbus's invasion of the island of Hispaniola, in the Native American genocide and enslavement, in African colonialization, in the rise and spread of Christianity, and in the transatlantic slave trade.

It even shows up in the Declaration of Independence. Rooted in John Locke's libertarian ideology, the Declaration of Independence asserts that "all men are created equal, that they are endowed by their Creator with certain unalienable rights . . . Life, Liberty and the Pursuit of Happiness."

Although the Declaration of Independence established the sovereignty of the thirteen original US colonies, its aspirations spoke solely to land-owning, white men. It did not apply to the 600-plus enslaved Africans Thomas Jefferson amassed over his lifetime, nor to the slaves of the other four slave-owning founding fathers, nor to the Native Americans living on the land these men claimed as their own. It did not apply to the founding fathers' white sisters, wives, mothers, and other female counterparts. Although these men and their influencers purported ideas of equality and liberty, there was a shared implication that such core values were only afforded to or deserved by white men. White supremacy—in the most literal understanding of that term—is at the political core of the United States. The founding fathers understood that their aspirations and freedom hinged upon a fierce guardianship, an active implementation of otherness. In order for the United States to employ a sense of superiority or dominance, one group had to exert control over others. That group was white men.

We can see this play out in the history, language, and values that marked the early decades of American life. American pioneers and political architects understood the power, utility, and convenience of widespread "othering"—it suited the maintaining of white supremacy under the guise of civility. These beliefs and values were explicitly and legally applied and acted upon from the arrival of the first settlers and, arguably, through the present. Think of the language around the birth and growth of the United States: "how the West was won" (from whom?), "manifest destiny" (whose destiny?), "the American dream" (whose dream?). Supremacy, conquering, and ownership of the other prop up the story.

Over time, this mentality helped shape US concepts of patriotism and nationalism. As early communication transitioned from a limited number of literate men who read and crafted news, to the mass distribution of information through use of the printing press for newspaper circulation, then radio and television, America's hegemony—"preponderant influence or authority over others"[6]—was developed through the spread of a specific set of shared culture, political thought, and values. Even as the demographics of the United States changed with the influx of immigrants from around the world, white men with power continued to control the narrative.

All of this background brings us to September 2001, the point at which we see how this underlying othering has influenced perceptions and policies related to refugees. After the 9/11 attacks on the Pentagon and the World Trade Center towers, President George W. Bush began a political and media campaign of anti-terrorism rhetoric based strongly on othering. His "War on Terror" was predicated on asking the American public, "Why do they hate us?" "They" are nearly 23 percent of the world's population, or about 1.6 billion individuals who identify as Muslim. But with one short question, the president turned all 1.6 billion persons into a single threatening presence. For most Americans, this translated to "They are not Christian and not white. They do not believe in liberty, freedom, and democracy. They are not like *us*." This us-and-them strategy constructed a perception of the strange foreignness of the Middle East and the global Muslim community. With this artificial barrier, a phantom fear was born, fear that led to widespread public and congressional support for the US invasion of Afghanistan and Iraq, which, arguably, led to the rise of ISIS and the Syrian civil war. The president's coded language began the process of cultural, social, and political distancing, setting an entire region at odds with American/Christian values.

As a result, otherness has permeated the ways refugees and other newcomers are considered and discussed in the United States. During the 2016 presidential election, newcomers were referred to in the press as *illegals, Muslims, Mexicans, rapists, bad hombres,* and *these people.* Such terms were often used broadly, lumping together those seeking political asylum, refugees, immigrants, foreign-born professionals, and individuals living in the United States temporarily. It didn't matter what the differences between them were—they were not *from* the US. This inaccurate and damaging terminology implies that all newcomers are the same and that all possess violent or extreme tendencies. It pits newcomers and their advocates against one another, prompting a tiered system of need and legitimacy—refugees are seen as victims of conflict, while others are opportunists. Neither is considered deserving of our resources needed to allow them entry into this country. Othering ensures that the public sees newcomers as something alien and unsafe. The pervasive political and social conversation about "maintaining US values" is code for keeping the United States white and Christian.

The othering narrative also distills the complexities of the refugee crisis into a singular binary conversation—refugees as a whole group are seen as either deserving of help or not.

I recall the moment I saw the image of Alan Kurdi, the deceased Kurdish Syrian toddler found washed ashore in Turkey, in my newsfeed in September 2015. This disturbing photo left an indelible impression on our collective global psyche. People grieved and were horrified to see that Alan resembled their own child, relative, or neighbor. At our national refugee resettlement headquarters, we fielded a slew of inquiries and offers from concerned and compassionate Americans: "Where should I send my donations?" "I have an empty bedroom! A Syrian family can come live with me!" "How can I help bring a Syrian family here to Montana?"[7] Local and national refugee resettlement offices noted a significant uptick in public inquiries, political support, cash and in-kind donations, and advocacy efforts pushing for increased US refugee support as a result of the conversations surrounding the horrific Syrian and global refugee crisis.

My US refugee protection colleagues applauded the renewed political commitments and the community support and conversations about welcome for refugees. Yet I joined other global refugee experts who wondered both silently and aloud, Would Americans and Europeans have reacted differently if Alan looked like he hailed from Burma? The Democratic Republic of Congo? Somalia? Was the image of a lifeless child on a Turkish beach sufficient to solicit such reactions and reconsiderations of not only the plight of Syrian refugees but the greater global refugee crisis as well? A resounding "yes, of course" is the simple, desirable answer. But since thousands of deceased African child and adult migrants had *already* washed ashore on Italian, Spanish, and North African beaches over more than a decade, it's hard to be sure.

Two years after the Kurdi news story, I stumbled upon a story about Samuel Kabangal, a four-year-old Congolese refugee. His body had also washed up on shore—in his case, at Cádiz, Spain, while his mother's washed up on an Algerian beach. Traveling from Kinshasa, he and his mother departed Morocco trying to reach Europe in search of medical treatment for Samuel's lung condition. A Cádiz priest who had worked with refugees for more than twenty-five years lamented the tragedy. An article in *The Guardian* reported on the priest's grief at the lack of attention these deaths brought: "For two days he waited for word of the tragedy to spread—and for the attendant outrage. When neither was forthcoming, he tweeted: 'The death of Alan, the little Syrian boy, moved the world. On Friday, the body of a young immigrant boy washed up on the coast of Cádiz and no one's saying anything.'"[8]

Alan's image and passing brought compassion and humanity back to the refugee conversation. It taught Americans and Western Europeans that their existing concepts of refugees and immigrants lacked nuance and understanding of global realities. Yet for the remainder of the world and for other refugees, it was a reminder that the valuation of lives remains a hierarchical affair.

WHOSE HISTORY?

The current pushback against refugee resettlement represents the collision of this tendency for othering with the long human history of migration. If every people group throughout history had just stayed put, the problem of othering might be nothing more than a quirk of the human condition. But when the "other" comes to our doorstep, we are faced with the dangerous implications of this need for hierarchy.

Humans move. Whether within neighborhoods, from state to state, or across oceans, human movement is the most constant and least contested historical spectacle. Human migration is a universal force driven by nature and the quest for survival. Historically, migration was considered through a binary lens—voluntary and involuntary. Voluntary migrants—people who choose to move or use their own agency to move—include explorers, students, academics, business people, and artists. Those with no choice or minimal agency include asylum seekers, slaves, survivors of trafficking, and refugees. Societies are formed when involuntary and voluntary migrants are mixed in with indigenous communities and sustained by their descendants. Of course, historically, that mix often becomes toxic fairly quickly.

European colonial efforts brought exploiters to the Americas in the mid-fifteenth century. Shortly after arrival, Europeans began a systematic extermination of indigenous populations in the United States, the Caribbean, and Central and South America, with more of the same in Africa, Asia, and Oceania. After Christopher Columbus's contested discovery of "India," or the present-day Dominican Republic, these European houseguests began centuries of what could politely be considered in current terms a flagrant display of bad manners.

Native American communities were systematically exterminated through forced relocation, enslavement, intentional exposure to infectious disease and alcohol, forced conversion and assimilation, and mass killings. Due to Columbus's failure to discover the anticipated riches of the New World, he took Native Americans instead of the gold and resources he and his Spanish sponsors had sought to secure. In an attempt to continue funding his expeditions, Columbus kidnapped and transported Native Americans back to Spain for enslavement and forced servitude. Between 2 and 5.5 million Native Americans were enslaved in North America and the Caribbean and shipped to Spain, Portugal, and North Africa for enslavement.[9]

As European imperialism and colonialism expanded in what would become the United States, so did settlers' need for expertise, labor, and resources. For the next 341 years, European settlers' greatest economic success was found in the transport, purchase, sale, and breeding of enslaved Africans brought to the Americas via the transatlantic slave trade. It is estimated that 12.5 million enslaved Africans were forcibly brought to the Americas during the legal slave trade,[10] with most shipped to the Caribbean and South America. Enslaved Africans, or African American labor, built and sustained early US agriculture, infrastructure, and colonial family life throughout fifteen US states and territories until the abolishment of slavery in 1865.

Africans and Native Americans were not the sole victims of servitude and European settlers' hierarchy. Working-class and poor whites were also brought to the New World to work—often alongside African slaves—to build the Americas. Like their Native American and African colleagues, the white working class derived from a sort of bondage. Having been sponsored for passage to America, poor whites were required to work off their debt. This resulted in the building of an indentured-servant class inferior to white aristocracy, yet more privileged than African and Native American slaves. European indentured servants also endured harsh work, poor conditions, and ill-treatment, yet their servitude was often time-bound and included a salary. Their descendants were considered white labor or "servants" and were ultimately afforded rights as members of the white, or European, community. Although not considered or treated as permanent property, their status cemented early European settlers' felt need to create and maintain a social hierarchy in the so-called New World.

From the 1880s through the 1940s, more than 40 million newcomers joined the earlier voluntary migration of Europeans and the forced migration of Africans to the United States.[11] A mix of migrants, refugees, students, professionals, family members, friends, and opportunists of various economic levels and from homelands across Africa, Asia, and Europe, they headed to major cities and ports: Boston, Chicago, the District of Columbia, Philadelphia, New Orleans, New York, and San Francisco. Over the course of the past two centuries, the demographics and ethnic makeup of the US have undergone dramatic shifts shaped by distinct waves of immigration. As the cultural, economic, political, and social landscape of the US changed and various immigration policies were implemented, some sought to activate our nation's Latin motto—*E pluribus unum,* or "Out of many, [we are] one."

Yet the illusion of oneness was selectively applied—many US citizens and newcomers never walked over a "welcome mat."

THE GREAT MIGRATION

I was leaving the South
To fling myself into the unknown . . .
I was taking a part of the South
To transplant in alien soil,
To see if it could grow differently,
If it could drink of new and cool rains,
Bend in strange winds,
Respond to the warmth of other suns
And, perhaps, to bloom.

—**Richard Wright**[12]

When I think about the current state of newcomer welcome and the global refugee crisis, I am always drawn back to the largest and longest internal migration and a key historical phenomenon in US history: The Great Migration.

From 1915 to 1970, more than six million descendants of African slaves, or African Americans, fled the South and moved north and west. According to journalist and migration scholar Isabel Wilkerson, the Great Migration surpassed the migrations of the 1850s Gold Rush in California and the 1930s Dust Bowl.[13] It can be considered one of the most complex and reverberating phenomena in US history.

There was no single push factor, or reason, why millions of African Americans "up and left" the South. Each migrant had his or her own narrative, trauma, agency, and reasons for flight, yet collectively, the factors told the story of the African American experience. It doesn't take long to see the connections between the Great Migration and experiences that lead to refugee migration today.

Thousands of African American patriots and veterans returned home from serving in World War I, World War II, or the Korean conflict, only to be ratcheted back to the everyday oppression and violence of the Jim Crow South. Veterans lamented that in Europe they were treated as men, but back

South. Veterans lamented that in Europe they were treated as men, but back home in (*insert any southern state here*) they were considered subhuman. Such treatment ranged from being verbally assaulted by white citizens to being overlooked for jobs or underpaid by white employers. Even worse, countless men were beaten, disrobed, and/or lynched for a perceived slight or out of white men's spite over a black man in uniform, decorated with medals of honor, and displaying signs of respect. As Wilkerson notes, "Some [African American veterans] survived the war only to lose their lives to Jim Crow."[14]

One of the most pervasive and terrifying aspects of the Jim Crow South was the indiscriminate lynching of black citizens. Sociologist Arthur Franklin Raper observed that within a thirty-year period, a black man or woman was hanged or burned alive every four days.[15] Wilkerson quotes historian Herbert Shapiro, who wrote that "all Southern blacks lived with the reality that no black individual was completely safe from lynching."[16] Fear, a psychological weapon of war for those engaging in domestic terrorism against blacks, was perpetuated by the resurgence of the Ku Klux Klan, often in collusion with local or state law enforcement. White citizens terrorized black communities and razed prosperous black towns like Tulsa, Oklahoma,[17] and Rosewood, Florida,[18] employing fire and bullets while law enforcement and the federal government looked the other way or assisted.

According to the 1951 United Nations Refugee Convention definition, millions of Southern blacks during this era would be considered refugees due to their sustained fear, persecution, and lack of protection by and from local, state, and federal governments. African Americans explicitly fled the South for the same reasons that refugees leave their countries: the US government repeatedly failed to protect and provide them with the same rights, access, services, acknowledgment, and respect granted to white citizens. Like some of the original American colonizers from England and, more recently, refugees from Bhutan, Eritrea, Somalia, and Syria, black Americans fled oppression and fear in the South, traveling at great cost and going to great lengths to reach safety. They clung to the hope that their lives and the lives of their children would be better. So they left.

The resettlement experiences of African Americans were similar to those of many refugees today. They were often met with discrimination, stereotypes, and skepticism from their new neighbors. Regardless of their physically grueling jobs with long hours and lower wages than their white counterparts. Black factory and railroad workers were often seen as competition for white Northerners and other European migrants. Housed in overcrowded and unsanitary tenement apartments, black newcomers often paid twice as much as white tenants for subpar housing in places like Chicago and New York. The trend of overcharging and underinvesting in majority–African American communities set the economic tone for future discriminatory housing practices and redlining that still reverberates today.

And yet, the Great Migration also serves as something of a blueprint, or societal doppelganger, for how the US can, and often does, welcome newcomers. African Americans' arrival and resettlement in the North and West transformed the cultural, economic, political, and social urban landscape into a form that remains visible in today's cities and metropolitan areas. The Great Migration nudged the Civil Rights movement along and paved the way for nationwide political and social reform. African Americans' experiences and the structures subsequently put in place etched a well-worn resettlement path for non-native migrants from Asia, Africa, the Caribbean, and even Europe to follow. While current newcomers still face injustices, their experiences have context and an established precedent for how otherness plays out, as well as for successful methods to combat it.

THE ROOTS OF CHANGE

Whether examining the impact of otherness from the perspective of African Americans' Great Migration, Native Americans' experience, colonialism, or today's newcomer challenges, the act and implementation of othering is a losing game. It is equally damaging to both those who are treated as other and those who do the othering. It creates fear—a fear of the other, and fear of being the other at some point. Dismantling white hierarchy and supremacism might ultimately take as long as it took to construct it. Seems daunting, right? That said, there are tangible actions, attitudinal shifts, and reckonings that make room for healing, progress, and the deconstruction of both individual and systemic resistance to welcoming the stranger.

Over the past several years, I've visited various US communities where people are welcoming and supporting refugees. Some are diverse, liberal, well-resourced, and global in scale and focus, while others are more insular, well-resourced, and global in scale and focus, while others are more insular, working-class cities with mostly Christian residents and values. Regardless of their political or theological leanings, one shared component of successful refugee welcome and support is strongly intentional, strategic community engagement. Whether through community groups or local government and civic efforts, welcoming communities provide newcomers with financial and social support, resources, and services while engaging the established community in cultural literacy and opportunities for everyday interaction with refugees.

A pressing need is for citizen education and information-sharing. Arming individuals and communities with information, history, and perspective creates positive power. It allows communities to acknowledge the racism embedded in our American history and institutions without getting stuck in defensiveness. It challenges us to do better.

A few tips: To be a truly welcoming community, be responsible for your own self-education. Start a book club to read and discuss alternative perspectives on global and US history in order to forge a new kind of welcome experience for newcomers. Enroll in a course at your local educational institution or online. There is a growing body of literature that provides an understanding of refugees' experiences, journeys, and plight. There are also numerous narratives, studies, and accounts illustrating local newcomer successes and complexities. Discuss your takeaways, concerns, and conflicts with family, friends, colleagues, and neighbors. Seek out knowledge and information from trustworthy sources instead of relying on others to provide you with information. Cultivate a working knowledge of history and facts to counter assumptions, stereotypes, and opinions from community members and elected officials who want to perpetuate dangerous and misleading ideas.

As American individuals and communities continue to sort out their feelings about how and what they consider a satisfactory welcome, global conflicts still rage, refugees continue to flee, and newcomers to the US continue surviving, thriving, and contributing to their new homeland. Newcomers are represented at every level of local, state, and national governance. They are public school teachers, law enforcement officers, factory workers, business owners, professors, military officers, pastry chefs, retail managers, medal-winning Olympic athletes, journalists, humanitarians, stay-at-home parents, engineers, poets, pasta makers, pediatricians, religious leaders, and citizens. *They* are not other. *They* are just like *us*.

Halima Z. Adams is a forced migration and protection practitioner with more than fifteen years of multi-sector experience in humanitarian affairs, human rights, public diplomacy, and development in the United States and abroad. At Church World Service, she oversees monitoring and evaluation activities and gender equality initiatives for assessing newcomer resettlement and integration programs in the U.S. She has worked with refugees in England and Egypt. Some of her research, writing, and interests include: newcomer integration, the roles of migrant diasporas, transnationalism, migrant culture, and cultures of exile, and African American migration phenomenon in the U.S. Halima holds an M.A. in Forced Migration and Refugee Studies from the University of East London, and a B.S. in Public Relations and Political Science from Florida Agricultural and Mechanical University.

ENDNOTES

1   Ta-Nehisi Coates, "The First White President," *The Atlantic,* October 2017. https://www.theatlantic.com/magazine/archive/2017/10/the-first-white-president-ta-nehisi-coates/537909/.

2   *Mabrouk* is the Arabic word for "congratulations."

3   Alexa Liataud, "Mike Pence Loses Legal Battle to Keep Syrian Refugees Out of Indiana," *VICE News,* March 1, 2018. https://news.vice.com/en_us/article/59ka9a/mike-pence-loses-legal-battle-to-keep-syrian-refugees-out-of-indiana.

4   G. W. F. Hegel, *Phenomenology of Spirit,* trans. A. V. Miller (Oxford: Oxford University Press, 1977).

5   Edward Said, *Orientalism* (New York: Vintage Books, 1979).

6   *Merriam-Webster Online*, s.v. "hegemony," accessed April 6, 2018. Continually updated at http://unabridged.merriam-webster.com/collegiate/hegemony.

7   Gabriel Furshong, "The Montana Moms Who Decided Refugees Will be Welcome in Their City," *Yes Magazine*, July 3, 2017. http://www.yesmagazine.org/people-power/the-montana-moms-who-decided-refugees-will-be-welcome-in-their-city-20170703.

8   Sam Jones, "'He Was Just a Kid': The Boy Who Became a Symbol of Spain's Migration Crisis," *The Guardian,* January 26, 2018. https://www.theguardian.com/world/2018/jan/26/boy-symbol-spain-migration-crisis-samuel-kabamba.

9   Andrés Reséndez. *The Other Slavery: The Uncovered Story of Indian Enslavement in America* (Boston: Houghton Mifflin Harcourt, 2017).

10   Trans-Atlantic Slave Trade Database, http://www.slavevoyages.org/.

11   Joshua Zietz, "The Real History of American Immigration," *Politico Magazine*, August 6, 2017. https://www.politico.com/magazine/story/2017/08/06/trump-history-of-american-immigration-215464.

12   Richard Wright, *Black Boy (American Hunger): A Record of Childhood and Youth* (New York: Harper Perennial, 1993).

13   Isabel Wilkerson, *The Warmth of Other Suns* (New York: Vintage, 2010).

14   Wilkerson, 145.

15   Arthur F. Raper, *The Tragedy of Lynching* (Chapel Hill, NC: University of North Carolina Press, 1933).

16   Raper, 39.

17   Scott Ellsworth, *Death in a Promised Land: The Tulsa Race Riot of 1921.* (Baton Rouge, LA: Louisiana State University Press, 1982). In 1921, the affluent African American neighborhood in Tulsa, often called "the Black Wall Street," was attacked by local Tulsa residents and police when a young black man was accused of raping a white female elevator operator. Eyewitnesses claimed the police dispatched airplanes dropping firebombs on rooftops. The mob looted and burned residents' homes and businesses; 10,000 black residents were left homeless; 6,000 were arrested and detained; 800 were injured; and hundreds were killed. An estimated $1.5 million in real estate and $500,000 in personal property was lost. Black residents were never compensated for their losses. The massacre was only recognized and properly researched in 2001 in a report from the Oklahoma Commission to Study the Tulsa Race Riot of 1921.

18   Michael D'Orso, *Like Judgment Day: The Ruin and Redemption of a Town Called Rosewood* (New York: Grosset/Putnam, 1996). Rosewood was an independent, black community in Central Florida. In 1923, a white mob lynched a black Rosewood resident who allegedly had sexually assaulted a white woman. When armed black Rosewood residents rallied to defend their community against further violent attacks, a white mob attacked the residents and burned the entire town over the course of a week, pursuing the remaining black residents who sought safety in nearby swamps. Official reports stated that "several" black and white residents died in the massacre, while witnesses noted that as many as 150 residents died during the weeklong event. In 1994, the Florida legislature passed the Rosewood Compensation Bill, which included a $1.5 million settlement for Rosewood massacre survivors. Nine survivors were awarded $150,000 each.

6

LOOKING FOR HOME
CREATING COHESIVE COMMUNITIES

BY AUBREY LEIGH GRANT

In May of 1939, the SS *St. Louis*, a German transatlantic liner, reached Havana, Cuba. Aboard the ship were 937 Jewish passengers seeking refuge from the Third Reich. With Cuban landing certificates in hand, the goal of many on board was to wait safely there until they received US visas. But after reaching Havana, the majority of the passengers had their landing certificates and transit visas revoked due to political divisions in Cuba and were kept from disembarking.

After being ordered to leave Cuban waters, the captain of the SS *St. Louis* directed the ship north toward Miami. Those aboard held out hope that the ship would be allowed to dock in Florida, and that the US government would issue the passengers visas. The ship's refugees, who were so close to the United States that they could see Miami's lights, sent cables to President Franklin Roosevelt and the State Department. The Roosevelt administration never responded to the Jewish refugees' cries for help; however, a State Department official informed them that they must "await their turns on the waiting list and qualify for and obtain immigration visas before they [could] be admissible into the United States."[1] With the US government refusing to admit the refugees, the *St. Louis*'s captain had no option but to head back to Europe. Over the course of the return voyage, the Jewish Joint Distribution negotiated with Great Britain, the Netherlands, Belgium, and France, securing entry visas for all passengers. But when the Third Reich advanced into Western Europe, 532 SS *St. Louis* passengers would find themselves under Nazi control. Only 278 of them would survive the war.[2]

This dark moment in American history has not been forgotten. Since World War II, the United States has become a beacon of hope for the world's most vulnerable populations. The US is one of thirty countries that work with the United Nations High Commissioner for Refugees (UNHCR) to facilitate an international resettlement program around the world. But in 2016, this program resettled less than 1 percent of the world's displaced population—around 140,000 refugees.[3] Of these individuals, 84,995 were resettled in the United States through the US Resettlement Program (USRP).[4]

The strength of western democracies relies, in part, on the social cohesion of their populations: How do people of various backgrounds get along? How do they make decisions in light of cultural and individual differences? What helps them form communities out of disparate values, goals, and resources? These are big sociological questions with significant implications for refugee resettlement. In acknowledgment of that fact, a core part of resettlement is the process by which existing communities and newcomers adapt and transform to build group cohesion. Academic scholars have long theorized and debated "those phenomena which result when groups of individuals having different cultures come into continuous first-hand contact, with subsequent changes in the original culture patterns of either or both groups."[5] Over the last few years, our ideas about what successful social cohesion looks like, and what it takes to get there, have changed. Our ideas about what it means to welcome refugees have changed along with them.

NO EASY ENTRY

Every year, the US president, in consultation with Congress, sets a resettlement admissions ceiling, including quotas for the number of refugees from different parts of the world. These numbers are determined by world events, US foreign policy, and the level of need in a given year. For example, when a civil war breaks out somewhere in the world, the president might adjust the ceiling for the coming year to accommodate newly displaced citizens of that region. The ceiling was at its highest level in 1980 with 231,700 individuals permitted entry. In 2018, the ceiling was set at an all-time low of 45,000 individuals.[6] These numbers include people who arrive at US borders seeking asylum. Historically, the actual number of refugees admitted falls below the predetermined number.

The screening process that refugees go through in order to be accepted for resettlement is only one stage of the longer vetting process required for resettlement in the US. Once a refugee's case has been referred to the US, the refugee goes through another extensive vetting that takes, on average, two years to complete and combines the efforts of eight US federal agencies. The goal of the vetting process is to ensure that refugee claims are valid, that applicants pose no security risk, and that they carry no communicable or harmful diseases. By the time the process is completed, resettlement candidates have had extensive medical and health screenings, undergone evaluations through six security databases, had five background checks and four biometric security checks performed (biometric checks collect unique individual attributes such as fingerprints, photographs, and signatures, which are used for validation of one's identity and for additional security screenings), been through three in-person interviews, and had two additional inter-agency security screenings performed.[7]

In a 2017 *Washington Post* commentary, a former US Department of Homeland Security immigration agent, Natasha Hall, described the vetting process as extremely intensive, overwhelming, and traumatizing. Every interview is recorded and scrutinized, and the transcripts carefully analyzed and compared with one another and with any and all other documents gathered on an individual.[8] Throughout the process, officials look for any discrepancy that could potentially render someone inadmissible. These interviews require refugees to tell their stories of displacement multiple times, repeating the most traumatic experiences of their lives. Any missed detail or misremembered moment could mean the difference between qualifying for resettlement and being sent back to whatever temporary home they've found.

Once a refugee has been moved through the security screenings, they are lined up with refugee support centers set up by the US government to perform pre-departure medical screenings and paperwork.[9] Refugees undergo medical evaluations by an approved physician, tailored to ensure that certain conditions are met prior to their entering the United States. The secretary of Health and Human Services determines which diseases or illnesses pose a threat to US public safety and should be disallowed. These include communicable or infectious diseases; physical, mental, or behavioral illnesses; and substance abuse or addiction.[10] The medical information is collected by the Bureau of Population, Refugees, and Migration and entered into the Worldwide Refugee Admissions Processing System, both of which are part of the State Department. Refugee support centers then work with resettlement agencies and the United States Citizenship and Immigration Services to ensure proper placement of refugees based on their potential medical needs.[11]

Refugees enter the United States at designated ports of entry and are met by Center for Disease Control quarantine inspectors responsible for checking for infectious diseases and processing paperwork.[12] Additionally, refugee medical records are processed and logged into the CDC's Electronic Disease Notification system. These reports are passed along to the health department in the refugees' resettlement jurisdiction.

On paper this process seems straightforward and practical. However, finding a place of refuge is an arduous, protracted process. Families are often separated, and even after a safe place is found, reaching it is not guaranteed. In 2008, a refugee named Kibrom fled Eritrea and found shelter in the Shimelba refugee camp in Ethiopia. Securing temporary safety in the camp was bittersweet, as Kibrom was forced to leave his wife and three children behind in Eritrea. Over the course of six months, Kibrom's wife, Kewanit, was able to flee to the Mai Aini refugee camp in Ethiopia with the couple's two youngest children, Biniyam and Desset, and was eventually reunited with Kibrom in the Shimelba camp. The family's successful reunification was overshadowed by the anguish they felt for having to leave their four-year-old son, Finan, back in Eritrea with his maternal grandmother.

In 2013 against all odds, Kibrom, his wife, and their two children received the opportunity for resettlement in the United States. The family arrived in December after undergoing an extensive and invasive vetting process. However, their hearts remained in Eritrea with Finan. By January 2015, they were able to get Finan to the safety of an Ethiopian refugee camp under the supervision of his aunt. Kibrom promptly began filing the necessary paperwork to reunite Finan with his family in the US. As of January 2018, the Refugee Access Verification Unit had still not approved Kibrom's Affidavit of Relationship filing, leaving the prospect of a family reunion in limbo. Sadly, Kibrom and Finan's story is not unusual. The length of the process, the complexities of travel, and the limited resources available for refugees all mean that many refugee families have to make horrible choices about who will move on and who will stay behind.

THE 2017 TRAVEL BAN

The prolonged, vigorous vetting process has been exacerbated by the Trump administration's travel bans. The travel bans have led to unnecessarily lengthened and inhumane family separations that disproportionately affect children. In 2015, Amina and her two daughters found refuge in the United States.[13] Unfortunately, during the process Amina had to part ways with her three-year-old son, Mohamed. From the moment she arrived in the US, Amina worked to satisfy all the legal requirements to facilitate Mohamed's resettlement. As they waited for a reunion with him, Amina and her daughters made a new life for themselves in Ohio. On January 27, 2017, the recently inaugurated president issued an executive order barring the admission of individuals from seven predominantly Muslim countries and suspending the US Refugee Resettlement Program for 120 days, leaving families like Amina's stuck with no other option than to wait and hope the president would change his mind and restart the program. Beyond the initial travel ban, the US Refugee Program has been further impeded since early 2017 as various executive orders and pieces of administrative guidance have successfully prevented immigration and refugee resettlement for some of the world's most vulnerable people.

Amina, distraught by the endless separation, flew to Kenya in August of 2017 with the hopes of working with immigration personnel to bring her son home. However, she was unable to find anyone to help her and returned to the United States, still without her then five-year-old son. Having submitted all necessary paperwork and documentation, Amina continues to wait for a final decision by the United States Citizenship and Immigration Services. The story of Amina and Mohamed illustrates how biased policies have had devastating impacts on families for no other reason than to curry political points.

FINDING A HOUSE... AND A HOME

Once a refugee has been approved for resettlement in the United States, the process moves into the hands of one of the resettlement agencies that currently have a cooperative agreement with the US State Department. The agencies' national offices meet on a weekly basis with the State Department's Bureau of Population, Refugees, and Migration to assign cases to their affiliates in various resettlement communities based on case management capacity, family ties, local service capabilities, and population demographics. Once a case has been allocated and confirmed by a local office, case files are passed along so pre-arrival planning can begin. When possible, family members already in the area or volunteers are used as resettlement "co-sponsors" to help affiliates with the reception, placement, and integration of refugees.

When a refugee arrives in the United States, they are guaranteed a basic set of services for a minimum of thirty days. Upon arrival at the airport of final destination, refugees are welcomed by volunteers or resettlement agency staff, who escort them to their new home, provide them with a warm meal, and provide a basic safety orientation. While this might sound very official and somewhat perfunctory, anyone who has volunteered to welcome refugees at an airport reception will never forget the sight of individuals arriving, exhausted yet excited, in their new home with nothing more than a personal bag and the white International Migration Organization plastic bag that carries all their personal documents. Volunteers are often humbled and moved by the experience.

Resettlement agency staff work with the community to ensure that refugees have appropriate clothing and home furnishings, and that any immediate health concerns are quickly addressed. In the following days, refugees undergo an intensive schedule of orientations and enrollments. This standardized process is tightly monitored by the USRP and follows a strict timeline:

↳ Shortly after arrival, resettlement agencies facilitate a meeting to create a case management plan and determine which financial assistance program is most appropriate.

↳ Within seven days of arrival, the resettlement agency is responsible for ensuring that a refugee—referred to by resettlement agencies as the client—has been registered to receive financial, medical, and nutrition assistance.

↳ Within ten days of arrival, refugees are registered with the Social Security Administration and enrolled in English language classes and employment programs.

↳ Within the first thirty days of a refugee's arrival, resettlement agencies are responsible for ensuring that they receive necessary identification documents and that minors have enrolled in a local school system.

↳ Over the thirty- to ninety-day period, organizations are responsible for carrying out resettlement orientations and providing cultural classes. During this timeframe, refugees become accustomed to institutions and structures within their new community. For example, they are taught how to navigate the local transportation and health care systems, and how to shop for groceries and other necessities. Outside of core services, resettlement agencies provide ongoing support as refugees work toward their ultimate goal, self-sufficiency. To facilitate this process, resettlement agencies work with the local community and partner with other organizations like churches, along with state and local governments when possible.

↳ On the ninetieth day after arrival, the local affiliate provides documentation and updates to their national agency regarding the self-sufficiency of their clients. The resettlement agency then provides this information to the Department of Health and Human Services' Office of Refugee Resettlement and the Department of State's Bureau of Population, Refugees, and Migration.

Shortly after graduating college, I began working with resettlement agencies through the AmeriCorps ACCESS program in North Carolina. One of my first tasks was to teach a group of refugees how to ride the bus. I had never ridden public transportation myself, other than on tourist trips to Washington, DC. To be prepared to teach the group of refugees how to ride, I first went to the bus station, bought tickets for everyone, and proceeded to ride the buses to their neighborhoods to pick them up. I was nervous about navigating the bus system and saw this as a glimpse of how the refugees likely felt about getting around their new community. Even now, it amazes me how quickly these newcomers learn to navigate public transportation without access to smartphones or computers, and in a new place with a different language.

There are often moments of humor and cultural awakening for volunteers working with newly resettled refugees. I remember driving with a group of Burmese refugees when we passed an opulent animal hospital. Suddenly, my passengers started chattering excitedly in their native language. The individual in the passenger seat turned toward me and asked if that building was a doctor's office for animals. When I responded yes, he turned back to his friends and relayed the information. When I asked what they were talking about, he responded that they had not believed him when he initially told them that the building was a hospital for dogs. They were stunned to see that an animal hospital here was nicer than hospitals for people where they came from.

The first months of the resettlement program are an emotional whirlwind. A refugee's new life in America starts out on a warm note, but as time progresses, refugees experience unique hardships. Over the coming days, months, and years, they face a difficult, uphill battle of making a new life for themselves, all the while recovering from the trauma that forced them from their home country. Over time, their experiences—bitter and sweet— create new memories, tying them to their new community. One man I know summed up his experience by saying, "After the first week, I was excited to finally be in the US, safely resettled and optimistic about the potential for my life here. After the first month, I was exhausted—physically and mentally—and longed to be home with my family and my way of life. After the first year, I felt optimistic once again about the new life I was making in my new home."

THE MOVE TOWARD INTEGRATION

Theories of social cohesion go back nearly a century. The first major theory scholars set forth to explain this process was assimilation. In 1930, sociologists in Chicago proposed the concept of assimilation to identify the transformation process that immigrants and their children experienced as they integrated into American society.[14] Classical assimilation theory defines it as a process through which "persons and groups acquire the memories, sentiments, and attitudes of other persons and groups and, by sharing their experience and history, are incorporated with them in a common cultural life."[15] Unfortunately, many of the original studies were ethnocentric and included elements of cultural or racial bias, which placed immigrants from African countries on lower tiers in a cultural hierarchy. Some scholars and factions of the American public viewed the distinct traits of newcomers as deficiencies that needed to be overcome in order for a group to properly assimilate. Over time, the concept of assimilation has been revised and modernized. Today, a new version of assimilation theory pulls from previous concepts and criticisms, but describes assimilation as a process that occurs at the group level rather than as an individual effort.

In contrast to the concept of assimilation, multiculturalism suggests the equality of all groups within society. Multiculturalism envisions a society separated by two domains: the public and the private. In the public domain, there is a singularly accepted culture and set of rights practiced by all people, regardless of their own cultural background. Distinct cultural norms are saved for the private domain.[16] As a model, multiculturalism seems to embrace diversity and enable newcomers to retain their ethno-cultural and religious distinctiveness by allowing minority groups representation in political, economic, cultural, and linguistic facets of life. At the same time, the culture as a whole resists leaning too far toward one dominant cultural expression.

Over time, the concepts of assimilation and multiculturalism have become popular models of how best to create policy around refugee resettlement. The result has been a blend of the two. But neither model has proven adept at fully helping us identify or create true social cohesion either at the community level or at the public policy level. As a result, refugee policy and practice have begun to move in a new direction, one that centers on integration.

Integration is an umbrella concept that explains the labyrinth of policies and practices governments use to build social cohesion. Generally, integration is viewed as a two-way process in which both native and newcomer populations make accommodations for one another and create a new, socially cohesive society.[17] Within this broad concept is the view that governments can facilitate integration by creating policies that enable society to achieve common goals and uphold community ideals.

Integration occurs in different spheres of society—political, economic, social, and cultural. Political integration refers to the process by which refugees become increasingly engaged in political participation. The three dimensions of political integration include 1) trust in democratic political institutions, 2) political participation, and 3) acceptance of and adherence to a state's democratic values.[18] Economic integration considers the newcomer's participation in the labor force and occupational mobility—can they grow into new jobs, change careers, advance in their field, etc.? Social and cultural integration consider measures of such phenomena as intermarriage between natives and immigrants and language proficiency.

It's one thing to talk about integration. It's another to put it into practice. There is no singular path or process by which integration occurs, and no guarantee it will go well. At a national level, solid policy has been found to directly impact refugee integration. The way national governments identify and implement integrational practices influences resettlement and welfare services available to refugees.[19] Specifically, factors such as inadequate housing, legal status, and extended time detained in screening and resettlement protocols can delay the integration process for refugees.[20]

For example, a refugee's legal status affects how they engage with their local community and what opportunities they have. As you can imagine, this has a tremendous influence on the refugee's integration.[21] When refugees arrive in the United States, they are given work authorization but don't have a permanent residency visa (that is, a "green card"). After living in the US for a year, refugees can apply for a permanent residency visa, and after living in the US for five years, they can apply for citizenship. Each of these benchmarks provides refugees with a different level of legal rights. In the meantime, however, their legal status often becomes an obstacle to community involvement, relationships, and other opportunities for true integration.

Ibrahim[22] was resettled from Cuba as a child in the 1990s. He grew up in the United States under the watchful eye of a foster family. Ibrahim excelled in school and became active in his community. After high school, he moved to New York to attend college and eventually graduated with a master's degree focusing on international relations. While in college, Ibrahim began working on his application for permanent residency. However, without money for an attorney, he filled out the paperwork on his own. Ibrahim's application had some inconsistencies that led to its denial. Meanwhile, during the application process, Ibrahim received a job offer from the State Department; however, the status of his application, and its eventual denial, prevented him from accepting the job. In fact, over the course of the next year he was unable to accept any full-time, career-oriented job. As a result, Ibrahim began working two part-time jobs. Eventually, he was able to save enough to hire a lawyer to help him with residency permit appeals, but ever since the submission of his initial application, Ibrahim has remained in limbo. Despite his graduate-level education, he has been unable to begin his career and has juggled numerous jobs to pay for his regular living expenses and his legal fees. Ibrahim's legal status has limited his ability to fully participate in his community and has hindered his integration.

It might seem like simply removing barriers through social or economic programs would lead to faster, more effective integration for refugees. But researchers have been studying Norwegian and Swedish welfare refugee integration programs and have found just the opposite: that, in fact, extensive integration assistance has a limited impact on initial inequalities between refugees and the general population.[23] While it would be wonderful to find a simple, effective model of integration, it's becoming clear that it must be viewed as a long-term, multifaceted process that leans more heavily on local communities than on government programs.[24]

THE ESSENTIAL ROLE OF COMMUNITY

The unique global work of refugee resettlement means that the thirty nations that work with the UNHCR often share research and insights about what works and what doesn't when it comes to integrating refugees into their new communities. As nations, we learn from one another and work together to create policies that allow refugees safe places to land, but that can also benefit receiving communities. A study involving Italy and the Netherlands helps us think about the ways refugees themselves define integration. The study encourages policy makers to consider the refugee's perspective, rather than simply treating inclusion as a policy goal.[25] In West Midland, UK, refugee integration was affected by the level of cohesion present in the receiving community—what kind of intergroup relationships they had, what existing prejudices had already created tensions, what sense of community identity existed.[26] With international research like this to look to, the US Office of Refugee Resettlement (ORR) in the Department of Health and Human Services has worked to improve funding and resettlement services available to local communities. Each state that resettles refugees has services tailored to their budget and available programs, but ORR works outside of this initial funding to give organizations access to competitive grants. The aim of these grants and the programs they fund is to move beyond the initial goal of self-sufficiency for refugees and help them truly become part of their communities in meaningful ways.

Of course, no grant or government program can replace the work of local citizens and organizations that walk alongside refugees. Moses H. Cone Memorial Hospital's Congregational Nurses program in Greensboro, North Carolina, offers a prime example of how partnerships can help refugees and communities overcome challenges and strengthen relationships. Navigating the American health care system can be challenging for any of us. It can be especially overwhelming for immigrants. Resettlement organizations in Greensboro were hearing from refugees that they were having difficulty accessing preventive health care services. In response, a local hospital, Moses Cone, began working with the community and resettlement agencies to identify ways to overcome barriers, such as bridging language differences and ensuring culturally appropriate care. As a result of this collaboration, Moses Cone allocated resources from their congregational nursing program to the resettlement community.[27] A part-time nurse was made available to refugees and resettlement agencies to provide information regarding preventive health care and to help navigate the local health care system. The program has allowed health providers and volunteers to pull together to provide health care services to refugees, thereby strengthening the health and well-being of the whole community. In addition, the program has educated both refugees and the local community on health tactics, drawing from both the strengths of the community and the knowledge refugees bring with them.

Communities across the United States have taken active roles in local refugee resettlement programs, viewing participation as something that makes life richer for everyone involved. Alice[28] is an Iraqi refugee resettled in Pennsylvania. A local resettlement agency was able to pair her with a group of volunteers from a local church who became her co-sponsors. They worked with Alice and the agency to ensure that she was receiving all of her government services, as well as to help her become self-sufficient. When Alice was offered a job that was going to interfere with her English language classes, her co-sponsors devised a solution that could benefit Alice and their entire congregation. They found an Arabic/English speaker willing to provide dual language classes that would allow Alice to continue learning English and would offer the congregation a chance to learn Arabic.

Community collaborations have long-term implications as well, preparing us to be responsive, respectful global citizens. In Baltimore, Maryland, the Refugee Youth Project is a community-based, collaborative program that brings together refugee children and volunteers from the local community. In the short term, the program helps refugee children with schoolwork and literacy skills. In the long term, it uses extracurricular activities to enhance educational and cultural experiences for refugee children, while engaging the community and strengthening its diversity and global capacity.[29]

For all the work international and federal agencies do to seek safety and stability for vulnerable displaced people, communities and local organizations play perhaps the most crucial role in welcoming refugees and encouraging cohesion. It's not easy, and it's not quick. Integration requires local communities to become actively engaged in the resettlement process. It asks them to build strategic partnerships and step out of existing patterns to stretch their communal capacity. And it requires them to draw upon their strengths to help "welcome the stranger" (see Matthew 25:35, 38). This is the work to which we are called. It's the work we must do.

Aubrey Grant is a doctoral student at George Mason University's Schar School of Policy and Government. Her research focuses on the role of public policy in addressing issues of immigration, forced migration, gender, and global health. Aubrey received her Master of Public Policy from American University and her Bachelor of Arts in Political Science from the University of North Carolina at Wilmington. Prior to graduate school, Aubrey worked as a case manager for a refugee resettlement organization in Greensboro, North Carolina. Aubrey has held various immigration advocacy and policy positions in Washington, DC.

ENDNOTES

1   "Voyage of the St. Louis," *United States Holocaust Memorial Muse*um, accessed January 20, 2018, https://www.ushmm.org/wlc/en/article. php?ModuleId=10005267.

2   "Voyage."

3   United Nations High Commissioner for Refugees, "Resettlement in the United States," UNHCR, January 2018, http://www.unhcr.org/ resettlement-in-the-united-states.html.

4   Bureau of Population, Refugees, and Migration, "Fact Sheet: Fiscal Year 2016 Refugee Admissions," US Department of State, January 20, 2017, http://www.state.gov/j/prm/releases/factsheets/2017/266365. htm.

5   Marc Bornstein, *Psychological Acculturation: Perspectives, Principles, Processes, and Prospects*, (Routledge, 2013), 38.

6   "U.S. Annual Refugee Resettlement Ceilings and Number of Refugees Admitted, 1980–Present," Migration Policy Institute, https://www. migrationpolicy.org/programs/data-hub/charts/us-annual-refugee-re-settlement-ceilings-and-number-refugees-admitted-united.

7   "Resettlement in the United States," UNHCR, accessed April 29, 2018, http://www.unhcr.org/en-us/resettlement-in-the-united-states.html.

8   Natasha Hall, "Refugees Are Already Vigorously Vetted. I Know Because I Vetted Them," *Washington Post*, February 1, 2017, https:// www.washingtonpost.com/posteverything/wp/2017/02/01/refugees-are-already-vigorously-vetted-i-know-because-i-vetted-them/.

9   Donald M. Kerwin, "The Faltering U.S. Refugee Protection System: Legal and Policy Responses to Refugees, Asylum Seekers, and Others in Need of Protection," Migration Policy Institute, May 2011, https:// www.migrationpolicy.org/research/faltering-us-refugee-protection-sys-tem.

10   Mi-Kyung Hong et al., "Refugee Policy Implications of U.S. Immigra-tion Medical Screenings: A New Era of Inadmissibility on Health-Re-lated Grounds," *International Journal of Environmental Research and Public Health* 14, no. 10 (October 2017), https://doi.org/10.3390/ ijerph14101107.

11   Kerwin, 11.

12   Alfredo E. Vergara et al., "A Survey of Refugee Health Assessments in the United States," *Journal of Immigrant Health* 5, no. 2 (April 1, 2003): 67–73.

13   Nick Miriello and Keegan Hamilton, "Trump Is Quietly Winning His War Against Refugees," *VICE News*, February 2, 2018, https://news.vice.com/en_us/article/xw4e9a/trump-is-quietly-winning-his-war-against-refugees.

14   Rogers Brubaker, "The Return of Assimilation? Changing Perspectives on Immigration and Its Sequels in France, Germany, and the United States," *Ethnic and Racial Studies* 24, no. 4 (January 1, 2001): 531–548; Richard Alba and Victor Nee, "Rethinking Assimilation Theory for a New Era of Immigration," The International Migration Review 31, no. 4 (1997): 826–874.

15   Richard Alba and Victor Nee, "Rethinking Assimilation Theory for a New Era of Immigration," *The International Migration Review* 31, no. 4 (1997): 828.

16   John Rex, *Ethnic Minorities in the Modern Nation State: Working Papers in the Theory of Multiculturalism and Political Integration, Migration, Minorities, and Citizenship* (Basingstoke, UK: Palgrave MacMillan Press, 1996).

17   Terri E. Givens, "Immigrant Integration in Europe: Empirical Research," *Annual Review of Political Science* 10, no. 1 (2007): 72; Patrick Ireland, Becoming Europe: Immigration Integration and the Welfare State (University of Pittsburgh Press, 2004), 15.

18   Jean Tillie, "Social Capital of Organisations and Their Members: Explaining the Political Integration of Immigrants in Amsterdam," *Journal of Ethnic and Migration Studies* 30, no. 3 (May 2004): 530.

19   Deborah Phillips, "Moving Towards Integration: The Housing of Asylum Seekers and Refugees in Britain," *Housing Studies* 21, no. 4 (July 1, 2006): 539–53; Diane Sainsbury, "Immigrants' Social Rights in Comparative Perspective: Welfare Regimes, Forms in Immigration and Immigration Policy Regimes," *Journal of European Social Policy* 16, no. 3 (August 1, 2006): 229–44.

20   Phillips, 539–53; David Mullins and Pat A. Jones, "Refugee Integration and Access to Housing: A Network Management Perspective," *Journal of Housing and the Built Environment* 24, no. 2 (March 19, 2009): 103–25.

21   For more, see Portes and Rumbaut, Immigrant America; Sylvie da Lomba, "Legal Status and Refugee Integration: A UK Perspective," *Journal of Refugee Studies* 23, no. 4 (December 1, 2010): 415–36; Hana E. Brown, "Refugees, Rights, and Race: How Legal Status Shapes Liberian Immigrants' Relationship with the State," Social Problems 58, no. 1 (2011): 144–63.

22   Name and identifying details have been changed.

23   Marko Valenta and Nihad Bunar, "State Assisted Integration: Refugee Integration Policies in Scandinavian Welfare States: The Swedish and Norwegian Experience," *Journal of Refugee Studies* 23, no. 4 (December 1, 2010): 463–83.

24   Kathleen Valtonen, "From the Margin to the Mainstream: Conceptualizing Refugee Settlement Processes," *Journal of Refugee Studies* 17, no. 1 (March 1, 2004): 70–96, https://doi.org/10.1093/jrs/17.1.70.

25   Maja Korac, "Integration and How We Facilitate It: A Comparative Study of the Settlement Experiences of Refugees in Italy and the Netherlands," *Sociology* 37, no. 1 (February 1, 2003): 51–68.

26   Clare Daley, "Exploring Community Connections: Community Cohesion and Refugee Integration at a Local Level," *Community Development Journal* 44, no. 2 (April 1, 2009): 158–71, https://doi.org/10.1093/cdj/bsm026.

27   "Congregational Nurse Program," Cone Health, accessed January 21, 2018, https://www.conehealth.com/wellness/community-resources/congregational-nurse-program/.

28   Name and identifying details have been changed.

29   "Refugee Youth Project," Baltimore City Community College, accessed January 21, 2018, http://www.refugeeyouthproject.org/.

7

WHERE DO WE GO FROM HERE?

SEEKING A CHRIST-LIKE RESPONSE TO THE REFUGEE CRISIS

BY MATTHEW SOERENS

The refrain of a favorite Sunday school song from my childhood instructs that the way to "be happy in Jesus" is to "trust and obey." When it comes to our approach to refugees, though, I fear that the church in the United States has too often not obeyed the many biblical commands to love, welcome, and serve vulnerable immigrants: a recent survey of Protestant church leaders in the US found that just 8 percent said their congregation was actively involved in serving refugees within their community.[1] While some churches are responding heroically in the midst of a global refugee crisis, including many at the heart of the crisis in the Middle East and Africa, most American churches are unengaged. I believe the root of our failure to obey this biblical mandate is a failure to *trust*. Our actions, or lack thereof, are a direct consequence of the dispositions of our hearts and minds.

The attitudes of many Christians—like many other Americans—toward refugees are informed by a sense of fear: though they may feel compassion for those forced by persecution to flee their countries, many are also quick to cite concerns about terrorism, scarce resources, and cultural change. These concerns are so widespread that most white Protestant Christians (both mainline and evangelical) told pollsters in 2017 that they supported a total halt to refugee resettlement to the United States. (Ethnic minorities and those of other religious traditions, notably, were much less likely to express this view).[2]

As you know from the previous chapters, there are good, data-based reasons we can trust the thorough vetting process that the US government already has in place to screen refugees, a process that generally takes at least eighteen months, and sometimes much longer. To recap, the US refugee selection and vetting process involves a coordinated effort between various departments of the federal government and includes in-person interviews with trained officers of the Department of Homeland Security, as well as various background and medical checks. Our government ultimately selects just a small fraction of 1 percent of the world's refugees to make the cut and be welcomed to the United States. This careful and selective process has a remarkably strong record: Of the roughly three million refugees resettled to the United States since the Refugee Act was passed into law in 1980, not a single one has taken an American life in a terrorist attack.[3]

Similarly, there are good reasons to trust the conclusions of economists, who have found that, contrary to the perception that assisting refugees is too costly for the United States, refugees actually have a significant positive impact on the US economy. Refugees, like other immigrants, contribute as consumers, adding to the economy as they buy groceries, smartphones, cars, and homes. They also pay their taxes. While they receive some limited governmental assistance to get on their feet, within a generation they are paying *in* significantly more than they have ever received. A study by economists at the University of Notre Dame finds that twenty years after arrival, the average refugee adult has contributed $21,324 more in taxes than the combined cost of their resettlement assistance and any public benefits for which they have qualified.[4]

For Christians, though, our trust ultimately shouldn't be in the US government, nor in economists. We are commanded repeatedly in the Scriptures to put our trust in God. "Trust in him at all times, O people;" the psalmist writes, "God is a refuge for us" (Psalm 62:8). If we are obedient to the many commands of Scripture to love, welcome, and seek justice for refugees and other immigrants, we can trust in God's protection and provision, rather than act out of fear.

In the US context, the evidence suggests there is very little reason to fear refugees. But even if there were significant threats to our safety—as is the case for Christians in some other parts of the world, where the asylum-seekers they serve have not necessarily been carefully vetted—Christians should still resist acting out of fear, especially in the face of this clear biblical call. We would do well to emulate the faith of King David: "In God I trust; I am not afraid; what can flesh do to me?" (Psalm 56:4).

This radical trust in God allows us to respond fearlessly to the commands of Scripture. We see it in the parable of the Good Samaritan, Jesus' explanation of what it means to fulfill the Greatest Commandment (Luke 10:25-37). In this story, the priest and the Levite, religious leaders of the time, were afraid—and not without reason, at least from a human perspective. As Martin Luther King Jr. observed just days before he would lose his own life as he obediently trusted God's call:

> And you know, it's possible that the priest and the Levite looked over that man on the ground and wondered if the robbers were still around. Or it's possible that they felt that the man on the ground was merely faking. And he was acting like he had been robbed and hurt, in order to . . . lure them there for quick and easy seizure. And so the first question that the priest asked—the first question that the Levite asked was, "If I stop to help this man, what will happen to me?"[5]

But the Samaritan—the hero of this story and Jesus' model of neighborly love—takes a different approach. He responds out of compassionate obedience rather than fear. King suggests that as the Samaritan sees the man beaten by the side of the road, he asks, "If I do not stop to help this man, what will happen to *him*?"[6]

It's worth noting that *good Samaritan* would have been an oxymoron for Jesus' Jewish listeners, who generally viewed Samaritans as heretical foreigners. For example, when they were looking to insult Jesus, some of Jesus' critics accused him of being "a Samaritan and [having] a demon" (John 8:48), and two of Jesus' closest disciples seemed very eager to call down fire on an entire Samaritan village (Luke 9:54). But Jesus rebuked them—in fact, his interactions with Samaritans were consistently countercultural, recognizing the dignity and virtue of people whom many in his society despised and saw as a menace. To make the Samaritan the good guy in this story is not only an admonition of the instinct for self-protection shown by the priest and the Levite; it's also a critique of the very idea that a foreigner is subhuman or incapable of being an instrument of God's love and compassion.

If the church in the United States is to marshal a Christ-like response to the global refugee crisis, we'll need to emulate the Good Samaritan, not the priest and the Levite who could only think of their own well-being. We have to trust God enough that we focus on the plight of refugees, rather than solely on ourselves and on the perception of risk that elicits fear. The muscle of trust is strengthened by remembering the many promises of God's presence with us, the repeated commands throughout the Bible to not betray the refugee (Isaiah 16:3) but to love and seek justice for the foreigner who resides among us (Deuteronomy 10:18-19), and the life of Jesus, who consistently interacted with those on the margins of society in ways that recognized their dignity, value, and potential.

MOVING THE CHURCH TO ACTION

Turning our own hearts and minds toward compassion and care for refugees is obviously a huge step toward living out the biblical command. But local congregations also play a critical role in helping the broader community develop attitudes toward refugees that are biblically informed, grounded in the facts, and ultimately reflective of mutually transformational relationships between refugees and members of the communities that receive them. As one friend told me recently, pastors tend to have, at most, one or two hours per week to influence their congregants' thinking on refugee and immigration issues, while cable news and social media have the rest of the week. Whether you're a pastor or a parishioner, it can feel overwhelming and intimidating to challenge the attitudes so many Americans have absorbed from media narratives about refugees that seem designed to invoke fear. But that's precisely why it's so vital that local churches engage the topic, lest we outsource discipleship to the political pundits. This is what it means to be the church.

Within the church, discipleship is the work of the whole congregation. For pastors, it might mean preaching on the many biblical passages that speak directly to God's concern for refugees and other immigrants and on the heroes of the biblical narrative who were themselves forced to flee to foreign lands to escape persecution, including Jesus himself. For congregants, it could look like a push for Sunday school and adult education classes that create opportunities to more deeply engage the issue from a biblical perspective and address common security, economic, and cultural concerns and misconceptions head-on.[7]

Perhaps the most effective way to truly engage your community of faith in a move toward involvement in the lives of refugees is to be exposed to the stories of refugees themselves. At the corporate level, churches can open their pulpit to a guest pastor who is a refugee. The church can provide opportunities for refugees living in their community to share their personal testimonies during a worship gathering. Though not a true substitute for in-person interaction with someone who has lived the refugee experience, films and books can also help develop empathy among American Christians who simply have very little understanding of the persecution and loss that refugees have been forced to endure.

I believe that, if the church in the United States is to be freed from fear, we need to start with a firm foundation in the Word of God. But knowing that the Bible commands us repeatedly to welcome and love refugees and other foreigners is not enough: we are compelled to "be doers of the word, and not merely hearers who deceive [ourselves]," (James 1:22).

PRACTICAL WAYS TO WELCOME REFUGEES

Whether by bringing a meal to a refugee in your community or organizing a fund drive for refugees on the other side of the world, everyone can find a way to follow the biblical command to care for displaced people. Resettlement and relief agencies around the globe run on the power of volunteers.

SERVING AND BEFRIENDING REFUGEES RESETTLED TO THE UNITED STATES

One of the most straightforward ways for individuals or small groups to get involved is to connect with a local refugee resettlement agency. Each refugee resettled by the US State Department is assigned to a local agency affiliated with one of the nine national refugee resettlement organizations, most of which are faith-based organizations such as Lutheran Immigration and Refugee Services, Church World Service, World Relief, and the US

Conference of Catholic Bishops. As you now know, these resettlement organizations are responsible for helping refugees through at least the first several months of their life in the United States, including securing and furnishing housing, ensuring that each individual receives their Social Security card and registers for public benefits that they will rely on for at least the first few months, helping adults to find jobs, helping children to register for school, and helping with the complex process of cultural adjustment.

No resettlement agency accomplishes all of these tasks on its own: its staff relies heavily on volunteers, as well as on both monetary and in-kind donations from community members, churches, foundations, and others. One of the most common needs is for individual volunteers who can serve as relational connections for newly arrived refugees. In some cases, volunteers assist caseworkers or other agency staff with specific resettlement tasks, such as airport pickups, transportation, or apartment setups. One of the most vital roles for volunteers, though, is simply providing friendship— many refugees arrive in the country knowing no one at all. It's not hard to imagine the isolation and loneliness any one of us would feel if we found ourselves in a foreign country where we didn't speak the language and didn't know a soul. A friend who will visit on a regular basis, have the patience to be present even through the awkwardness of a language barrier, and help them learn an entirely new culture is a vital human connection in an incredibly stressful time.

Not surprisingly, these friendships often become long-term relationships. The integration process of making a life in a new community can take years, and most resettlement agencies are only able to provide resources for a limited time. Church-based volunteers who build genuine friendships with refugees can help well beyond the initial resettlement period and be an essential bridge to a refugee's full integration into their new home. Like any friendship, these relationships tend to change with time: when refugees first arrive, they have a host of needs, but the longer they are in the country, the more economically self-sufficient and culturally competent they become. Still, on the long journey along this road, refugees, like everyone else, need friends.

In addition to these individual efforts, many churches involve the whole congregation in the resettlement process by holding collection drives for the household items a refugee family will need when they first arrive. For example, Lakeland Community Church in Lee's Summit, Missouri, recently encouraged their congregants to put together "Welcome Kits" for each room of a refugee family's apartment—a kitchen kit including pots, pans, dishes, and silverware; a bedroom kit with sheets, blankets, and pillows; and a bathroom kit including toilet paper, soap, shampoo, towels, and a bath mat. They eventually collected more than sixty kits, worth about $7,000, which they donated to a resettlement agency. Lakeland pastor Martha Gillilan says she believes that faith communities have a unique mandate to help refugees as they first arrive, asking, "If not the church, then who?"[8]

Church-based volunteers can also help with English language acquisition. While refugees arriving in the United States come from diverse backgrounds and some may already speak English, most—about two-thirds of refugees who have arrived in recent years—speak no English at all upon arrival, and only 7 percent of refugees say they spoke English well upon arrival.[9]

Many churches have offered classes for those learning to speak, read, and write English. For example, Faith Church on the north side of Indianapolis, Indiana, began offering English classes in 2005, when they noticed that a significant number of refugees had been resettled in apartment complexes close to their church building.[10] Roughly ninety volunteers run the program that has grown to serve nearly 200 adults and 150 children from more than thirty countries of origin on a regular basis. To ensure a high quality of language instruction, the church has partnered with a college to develop a six-week training course in English language instruction for all of its teachers.

When Faith Church's English classes first began, some in the congregation were uncomfortable with refugees and other immigrants in "their" space. But as more and more church members became volunteers, built personal relationships with the refugee participants, and heard testimonials from the program's students, the congregation has come to embrace the ministry enthusiastically. Now, about one-fifth of the church's members are actively involved in the program. Dawn Waltz, a longtime volunteer with the program, says, "I feel like I travel around the world every Tuesday night."

SERVING REFUGEES OUTSIDE THE UNITED STATES

Even before the dramatic cuts to refugee resettlement enacted by the Trump administration, the vast majority of the world's displaced people were never considered for resettlement to the United States. In fact, the significant majority have never had the option of being resettled to the US, Canada, or a European country: 84 percent of the world's refugees live in developing countries, generally in a country neighboring the one they were forced to flee.[11]

While we can and should serve the refugees who arrive in our own communities—and can advocate for a higher share of the world's refugees to be given that opportunity—the church in the West must also advocate for and provide tangible help to the majority of the world's refugees who live elsewhere, generally in the difficult conditions of a refugee camp or in an urban area, struggling to make ends meet as they pay for their own rent but are not authorized to work.

Churches in the West—and the individuals within them—can provide vital financial support for churches, ministries, and organizations directly responding to the human needs—food, lodging, health care, trauma counseling—of the millions of individuals who have been forced to flee their homes. The sad reality is that refugee crises are not short-term disasters. They are protracted situations in which displaced persons end up spending many years, or even multiple generations, unable to safely return to their countries of origin. Because of this, many organizations also focus on economic, social, and spiritual development programs. Others focus on the root issues of conflict, marginalization, and poverty that tend to precede situations of forced migration, aiming to stop a new refugee crisis before it begins.

In addition to providing financial support, some individuals from churches in the United States have given of their time, serving in refugee camps either in permanent or short-term ministry roles. Beyond the assistance they provide, individuals who have spent even a short time serving in a refugee camp tend to be among the most passionate advocates for refugees when they return to their home churches, having personally witnessed the desperate conditions in which many refugees live.

RAISING OUR VOICES

This kind of advocacy points to another critical role churches can play in the lives of refugees. For decades, the US refugee resettlement program enjoyed broad bipartisan support in Congress. But in the past few years, a media narrative has taken root that (inaccurately) conflates refugees with terrorism. In response to their constituents' fears, many members of Congress have become wary of supporting refugee resettlement.

President Trump, whose campaign for the presidency in 2016 included strong criticisms of refugee resettlement, has employed the significant authority over refugee resettlement delegated to the president by the Refugee Act of 1980 to dramatically reduce the number of refugees allowed into the United States. In 2017, less than 34,000 refugees were resettled in the US, down from nearly 100,000 the previous year and more than 200,000 in 1980.[12] Concurrently, the Trump administration has proposed dramatic budget cuts to foreign aid, including support for refugees living abroad.[13]

These changes have brought questions of public policy to the forefront and have made advocacy an increasingly important way in which Christians can stand with refugees. One of the best definitions of *advocacy* is found in Proverbs 31:8, which instructs us, "Speak out for those who cannot speak for themselves, for the rights of all the destitute." Of course, refugees *can* speak for themselves—and we would do well to listen to them. But only US citizens can vote in US elections, so the voices of Americans within US churches are far more likely to influence the direction of US policies than those of non-citizens. We are called to be stewards of the influence that God has entrusted to us, using it to ensure a better situation not just for ourselves and our families, but also for those who are vulnerable around the world, and whom our faith teaches us to love as our neighbors.

Many local churches are, understandably, wary of engaging political issues, wary of alienating congregants or distracting from the gospel message. But when the Bible speaks clearly to a topic—as I believe it does to the topic of refugees—our churches must engage it as well, even when that involves taking part in conversations about public policy issues. We can discuss policies without becoming partisan, letting the Scriptures—rather than the campaign platform of any political party or candidate—be our guide. Ultimately, policy decisions directly impact people, and our claim to love our neighbor rings hollow if we are unwilling to leverage the influence entrusted to each of us as citizens in our democratic system of government.

Many Christian leaders have spoken up in the public sphere on behalf of refugees. In January 2017, in the hours and days following the first of several executive orders that placed a temporary halt on the US refugee resettlement program, staff and volunteers of the mainline Protestant-affiliated Church World Service helped mobilize protests in airports throughout the country.[14] A few weeks later, hundreds of evangelical pastors and leaders—representing every state in the country—signed a letter to President Trump and Vice-President Pence that ran as a full-page ad in the *Washington Post*, urging reconsideration of the policy. The following month, a similar letter organized by the Interfaith Immigration Coalition was signed by more than 5,000 religious leaders from throughout the country.

It's hard to measure precisely what impact these initiatives had on changing policy, but elected leaders do see initiatives like these as a measure of public opinion, particularly when led by influential faith groups that represent millions of voters. Just as importantly, these advocacy actions represent a form of public witness: if the church is silent as refugees and other vulnerable people are harmed by changes to policy, we are complicit, and those outside the faith may associate our indifference not only with the church but also with Christ.

While statements and protests from nationally prominent leaders are valuable, advocacy is not just for clergy; laypeople are often the most effective advocates. In the week preceding World Refugee Day in June 2017, for example, individuals—many of them mobilized by their local churches—made thousands of phone calls to the offices of their congressional representatives, urging the US government to welcome more refugees. Others met personally with their members of Congress, wrote letters, or used social media to share their concerns with their elected officials.

It's important to note that advocacy isn't limited to the federal level. While the president has concentrated authority in setting the level of refugee admissions, Congress sets the levels of funding for both overseas assistance and processing and resettlement for those coming to the United States. State and local policies also impact the level of support refugees receive once they arrive, including eligibility for public benefits, resources for finding work and learning English, educational support for refugee kids, and access to medical care, public transportation, and affordable housing. In fact, advocacy—whether telephone calls, emails, letters, or participation in public meetings—is often most effective at the most local level, where each elected official represents fewer constituents than those holding state or federal offices.

PRAYING FOR CHANGE

Jesus once told a parable of a widow who persistently pleads with an unjust judge for justice and, eventually, receives it because of her persistence (Luke 18:2-5). We, too, can and should persistently lobby human authorities for justice. But the point of Jesus' parable was not to be a good political advocate; it was to teach his disciples that we "should always pray and not give up" (Luke 18:1).

No matter where you live and no matter what resources you have, every Christian can pray for refugees. The scale of the crisis—an estimated 22.5 million refugees worldwide, higher than at any other point in recorded history[15]—is overwhelming, and our small actions can feel insignificant. But prayer reminds us that, no matter how large the giants of suffering and injustice may be, our God is greater.

As Henri Nouwen wrote, prayer is not only about changing external situations; it also is an instrument of our own transformation: "In the intimacy of prayer, God reveals himself to us as the God who loves all the members of the human family just as personally and uniquely as he loves us. Therefore, a growing intimacy with God deepens our sense of responsibility for others."[16] Prayer is not a substitute for our actions—for direct ministry in our own communities, financial support, and advocacy—but rather the fuel for these responses, building the trust in God that forms the foundation of our work.

Given media narratives that often tell an inaccurate or incomplete story about who refugees are, it is not surprising that many Christians—like many others in our society—feel a sense of fear when they think about refugee issues.

As Americans, we tend to place a high value on safety and security—"take care" and "be safe" are common threads in our vernacular. But we don't find those instructions in the Bible. Instead, we are repeatedly commanded to "take courage" and "be not afraid," as we follow where God leads us.

If and when we allow love, rather than fear, to guide our collective response to the global refugee crisis, we have the opportunity to witness how God works even in the midst of horrific suffering, bringing about redemption and wholeness as resilient people rebuild their lives. The church can reflect Jesus' love as we meet tangible needs, extend hospitality to newcomers, and advocate for just policies.

I believe that this is the church's moment to rise up.

Matthew Soerens serves as the US Director of Church Mobilization for World Relief and is the coauthor of Welcoming the Stranger: Justice, Compassion and Truth in the Immigration Debate *(InterVarsity Press, 2018) and* Seeking Refuge: On the Shores of the Global Refugee Crisis *(Moody Publishers, 2016). He has written on immigration and refugee issues for* The New York Times, The Washington Post, Christianity Today, Sojourners, *and various other publications. A graduate of Wheaton College and DePaul University's School of Public Service, Matthew lives in Aurora, Illinois with his wife, Diana, and their three children.*

ENDNOTES

1   LifeWay Research, "Pastor Views on Refugees: Survey of Protestant Pastors," January 2016, http://lifewayresearch.com/wp-content/up-loads/2016/02/Pastor-Views-on-Refugees-Final-Report-January-2016.pdf.

2   Pew Research Center, "In First Month, Views of Trump Are Already Strongly Felt, Deeply Polarized," February 16, 2017, http://www.peo-ple-press.org/2017/02/16/2-views-of-trumps-executive-order-on-travel-restrictions.

3   Tim Breene, "Separating Fact from Fear in the Refugee Ban," World Relief, February 15, 2017, https://www.worldrelief.org/blog/separat-ing-fact-from-fear-in-the-refugee-ban.

4   William N. Evans and Daniel Fitzgerald, "The Economic and So-cial Outcomes of Refugees in the United States: Evidence from the ACS," NBER Working Paper No. 23498 (June 2017), http://www.nber.org/papers/w23498.

5   Martin Luther King Jr., "I've Been to the Mountaintop" (public address), April 3, 1968, http://www.americanrhetoric.com/speeches/mlkivebeentothemountaintop.htm.

6   King.

7   A variety of tools are available to guide group study and discussion, including this book, and the "I Was a Stranger" Challenge Scrip-ture-reading guide, which invites participants to read one verse per day for forty consecutive days, focusing on God's heart for immigrants. To download the "I Was a Stranger" Challenge bookmarks for use in your church, or to find a digital version of the challenge through the popular YouVersion Bible app, visit www.evangelicalimmigrationtable.com/iwasastranger.

8   Emily McFarlan Miller, "'Jesus the Refugee': Churches Connect Christmas Story to Migrant Crisis," *USA TODAY,* December 23, 2016, https://www.usatoday.com/story/news/nation/2016/12/23/jesus-refu-gee-churches-connect-christmas-story-migrant-crisis/95787838/.

9   Randy Capps and Kathleen Newland, "The Integration Outcomes of U.S. Refugees: Successes and Challenges," *Migration Policy Institute*, June 2015, 11.

10   Stephan Bauman, Matthew Soerens, and Issam Smeir, *Seeking Refuge: On the Shores of the Global Refugee Crisis* (Chicago: Moody Publishers, 2016), 120-122.

11   United Nations High Commissioner for Refugees, "Global Trends: Forced Displacement in 2016," June 2017, http://www.unhcr.org/5943e8a34.pdf, 2.

12   Reports from US State Department Refugee Processing Center, accessed January 15, 2018, www.wrapsnet.org; for historical refugee arrival numbers, see Migration Policy Institute, "U.S. Annual Refugee Resettlement Ceilings and Number of Refugees Admitted, 1980–Present," https://www.migrationpolicy.org/programs/data-hub/charts/us-annual-refugee-resettlement-ceilings-and-number-refugees-admitted-united.

13   Bill Frelick, "Trump's Budget Cuts Would Cut Crucial Emergency Aid," Human Rights Watch, March 21, 2017, https://www.hrw.org/news/2017/03/21/trumps-budget-would-cut-crucial-emergency-aid. I have same questions here as for note 9.

14   Jack Jenkins and Emily McFarlan Miller, "Refugee Groups Fight Trump Travel Ban—and for Their Own Survival," *National Catholic Reporter*, February 17, 2018, https://www.ncronline.org/news/people/refugee-groups-fight-trump-travel-ban-and-their-own-survival.

15   United Nations High Commissioner for Refugees, "Global Trends: Forced Displacement in 2016," June 2017, http://www.unhcr.org/5943e8a34.pdf, 2.

16   Henri Nouwen, Donald McNeil, and Douglas Morrison, *Compassion: A Reflection on the Christian Life* (New York: Image Books, 1982), 109.

MORE RESOURCES ON THE REFUGEE CRISIS

RESETTLEMENT AND ADVOCACY AGENCIES:

Church World Service
www.cwsglobal.org

Episcopal Migration Ministries
www.episcopalmigrationministries.org

Lutheran Immigration and Refugee Service
www.lirs.org

Preemptive Love
www.preemptivelove.org

Refugee Council USA
www.rcusa.org

The Refugee Processing Center (RPC)
www.wrapsnet.org

UNHCR: The UN Refugee Agency
www.unhcr.org

U.S. Committee for Refugees and Immigrants
www.refugees.org

United States Conference of Catholic Bishops Migration and
Refugee Services
www.usccb.org

We Welcome Refugees
www.wewelcomerefugees.com

World Relief
www.worldrelief.org

NON-FICTION

Seeking Refuge: On the Shores of the Global Refugee Crisis
> by Stephan Bauman, Matthew Soerens, and Dr. Issam Smeir

The Displaced: Refugee Writers on Refugee Lives
> editor Viet Thanh Nguyen

The New Odyssey: The Story of the Twenty-First-Century Refugee Crisis
> by Patrick Kingsley

Voices from the "Jungle": Stories from the Calais Refugee Camp
> by Calais writers

Welcoming the Stranger: Justice, Compassion and Truth in the Immigration Debate
> by Matthew Soerens and Jenny Hwang Yang

We Wish to Inform You That Tomorrow We Will Be Killed with Our Families
> by Phillip Gourevitch

LITERATURE

A Long Way Gone: Memoirs of a Boy Soldier
    by Ishmael Beah

City of Thorns
    by Ben Rawlence

Exit West
    by Mohsin Hamid

The Last Illusion
    by Porochista Khakpour

The Kite Runner
    by Khaled Hosseini

The Beautiful Things That Heaven Bears
    by Dinaw Mengestu

The Refugees
    by Viet Thanh Nguyen

Say You're One of Them
    by Uwem Akpan

What Is the What
    by Dave Eggers

NOTES